PENGUIN PLAYS

THE PRICE

Arthur Miller was born in New York City in 1915 and studied at the University of Michigan. His plays include *All My Sons* (1947), *Death of a Salesman* (1949), *The Crucible* (1953), *A View from the Bridge* and *A Memory of Two Mondays* (1955), *After the Fall* (1963), *Incident at Vichy* (1964), *The Price* (1968), *The Creation of the World and Other Business* (1972), and *The American Clock* (1980). He has also written two novels, *Focus* (1945) and *The Misfits*, which was filmed in 1960, and the text for *In Russia* (1969), *Chinese Encounters* (1979), and *In the Country* (1977), three books of photographs by his wife, Inge Morath. His most recent works include a memoir, *Timebends* (1987), and the plays *The Ride Down Mt. Morgan* (1991), *The Last Yankee* (1993), *Broken Glass* (1993), which won the Olivier Award for Best Play of the London Season, and *Mr. Peters' Connections* (1998). He has twice won the New York Drama Critics Circle Award, and in 1949 he was awarded the Pulitzer Prize.

BY ARTHUR MILLER

DRAMA

The Golden Years
The Man Who Had All the Luck
All My Sons
Death of a Salesman
An Enemy of the People (*adaptation of the play by Ibsen*)
The Crucible
A View from the Bridge
After the Fall
Incident at Vichy
The Price
The American Clock
The Creation of the World and Other Business
The Archbishop's Ceiling
The Ride Down Mt. Morgan
Broken Glass
Mr. Peters' Connections

ONE–ACT PLAYS

A View from the Bridge, *one-act version, with* A Memory of Two Mondays
Elegy for a Lady (*in* Two-Way Mirror)
Some Kind of Love Story (*in* Two-Way Mirror)
I Can't Remember Anything (*in* Danger: Memory!)
Clara (*in* Danger: Memory!)
The Last Yankee

OTHER WORKS

Situation Normal
The Misfits (*a cinema novel*)
Focus (*a novel*)
I Don't Need You Anymore (*short stories*)
Theatre Essays
Chinese Encounters (*reportage with Inge Morath photographs*)
In the Country (*reportage with Inge Morath photographs*)
In Russia (*reportage with Inge Morath photographs*)
Salesman in Beijing (*a memoir*)
Timebends (*autobiography*)
Homely Girl, a Life (*novella*)

COLLECTIONS

Arthur Miller's Collected Plays (Volumes I and II)
The Portable Arthur Miller
The Theater Essays of Arthur Miller (*Robert Martin, editor*)

VIKING CRITICAL LIBRARY EDITIONS

Death of a Salesman (*edited by Gerald Weales*)
The Crucible (*edited by Gerald Weales*)

TELEVISION

Playing for Time

SCREENPLAYS

The Misfits
Everybody Wins
The Crucible

THE PRICE

A PLAY

Arthur Miller

PENGUIN BOOKS

PENGUIN BOOKS
Published by the Penguin Goup
Penguin Books USA Inc.,
375 Hudson Street, New York, New York 10014, U.S.A.
Penguin Books Ltd, 27 Wrights Lane,
London W8 5TZ, England
Penguin Books Australia Ltd, Ringwood,
Victoria, Australia
Penguin Books Canada Ltd, 10 Alcorn Avenue,
Toronto, Ontario, Canada M4V 3B2
Penguin Books (N.Z.) Ltd, 182-190 Wairau Road,
Auckland 10, New Zealand

Penguin Books Ltd, Registered Offices:
Harmondsworth, Middlesex, England

First published in the United States of America by
Viking Penguin Inc. 1968
Reprinted 1968
Published in Penguin Books 1985

ISBN 0-7394-0915-8

Printed in the United States of America

For Inge and Rebecca

THE PRICE

Characters

VICTOR FRANZ

ESTHER FRANZ

GREGORY SOLOMON

WALTER FRANZ

Act One

Today. New York.

Two windows are seen at the back of the stage. Daylight filters through their sooty panes, which have been X'd out with fresh whitewash to prepare for the demolition of the building.

Now daylight seeps through a skylight in the ceiling, grayed by the grimy panes. The light from above first strikes an overstuffed armchair in center stage. It has a faded rose slipcover. Beside it on its right, a small table with a filigreed radio of the Twenties on it and old newspapers; behind it a bridge lamp. At its left an old wind-up Victrola and a pile of records on a low table. A white cleaning cloth and a mop and pail are nearby.

The room is progressively seen. The area around the armchair alone appears to be lived-in, with other chairs and a couch related to it. Outside this area, to the sides and back limits of the room and up the walls, is the chaos of ten rooms of furniture squeezed into this one.

There are four couches and three settees strewn at random over the floor; armchairs, wingbacks, a divan, occasional chairs. On the floor and stacked against the three walls up to the ceiling are bureaus,

3

armoires, a tall secretary, a breakfront, a long, elaborately carved serving table, end tables, a library table, desks, glass-front bookcases, bow-front glass cabinets, and so forth. Several long rolled-up rugs and some shorter ones. A long sculling oar, bedsteads, trunks. And overhead one large and one smaller crystal chandelier hang from ropes, not connected to electric wires. Twelve dining-room chairs stand in a row along a dining-room table at left.

There is a rich heaviness, something almost Germanic, about the furniture, a weight of time upon the bulging fronts and curving chests marshalled against the walls. The room is monstrously crowded and dense, and it is difficult to decide if the stuff is impressive or merely over-heavy and ugly.

An uncovered harp, its gilt chipped, stands alone downstage, right. At the back, behind a rather makeshift drape, long since faded, can be seen a small sink, a hotplate, and an old icebox. Up right, a door to the bedroom. Down left, a door to the corridor and stairway, which are unseen.

We are in the attic of a Manhattan brownstone soon to be torn down.

From the down-left door, Police Sergeant Victor Franz enters in uniform. He halts inside the room, glances about, walks at random a few feet, then comes to a halt. Without expression, yet somehow stilled by some emanation from the room, he lets his gaze move from point to point, piece to piece, absorbing its sphinxlike presence.

He moves to the harp with a certain solemnity, as toward a coffin, and, halting before it, reaches out *and plucks a string. He turns and crosses to the dining-room table and removes his gun belt and jacket, hanging them on a chair which he has taken off the table, where it had been set upside down along with two others.*

He looks at his watch, waiting for time to pass. Then his eye falls on the pile of records in front of the phonograph. He raises the lid of the machine, sees a record already on the turntable, cranks, and sets the tone arm on the record. Gallagher and Shean sing. He smiles at the corniness.

With the record going he moves to the long sculling oar which stands propped against furniture and touches it. Now he recalls something, reaches in behind a chest, and takes out a fencing foil and mask. He snaps the foil in the air, his gaze held by memory. He puts the foil and mask on the table, goes through two or three records on the pile, and sees a title that makes him smile widely. He replaces the Gallagher and Shean record with this. It is a Laughing Record—two men trying unsuccessfully to get out a whole sentence through their wild hysteria.

He smiles. Broader. Chuckles. Then really laughs. It gets into him; he laughs more fully. Now he bends over with laughter, taking an unsteady step as helplessness rises in him.

Esther, his wife, enters from the down-left door. His back is to her. A half-smile is already on her face as she looks about to see who is laughing with him. She starts toward him, and he hears her heels and turns.

ESTHER: What in the world is that?

VICTOR, *surprised*: Hi! *He lifts the tone arm, smiling, a little embarrassed.*

ESTHER: Sounded like a party in here!

> *He gives her a peck.*

Of the record: What *is* that?

VICTOR, *trying not to disapprove openly*: Where'd you get a drink?

ESTHER: I told you. I went for my checkup. *She laughs with a knowing abandonment of good sense.*

VICTOR: Boy, you and that doctor. I thought he told you not to drink.

ESTHER—*laughs*: I had one! One doesn't hurt me. Everything's normal anyway. He sent you his best. *She looks about.*

VICTOR: Well, that's nice. The dealer's due in a few minutes, if you want to take anything.

ESTHER, *looking around with a sigh*: Oh, dear God—here it is again.

VICTOR: The old lady did a nice job.

ESTHER: Ya—I never saw it so clean. *Indicating the room*: Make you feel funny?

VICTOR—*shrugs*: No, not really—she didn't recognize me, imagine?

ESTHER: Dear boy, it's a hundred and fifty years. *Shaking her head as she stares about*: Huh.

VICTOR: What?

ESTHER: Time.

VICTOR: I know.

ESTHER: There's something different about it.

VICTOR: No, it's all the way it was. *Indicating one side of the room*: I had my desk on that side and my cot. The rest is the same.

ESTHER: Maybe it's that it always used to seem so pretentious to me, and kind of bourgeois. But it does have a certain character. I think some of it's in style again. It's surprising.

VICTOR: Well, you want to take anything?

ESTHER, *looking about, hesitates*: I don't know if I want it around. It's all so massive . . . where would we put any of it? That chest is lovely. *She goes to it*.

VICTOR: That was mine. *Indicating one across the room*: The one over there was Walter's. They're a pair.

ESTHER, *comparing*: Oh ya! Did you get hold of him?

VICTOR—*rather glances away, as though this had been an issue*: I called again this morning—he was in consultation.

ESTHER: Was he in the office?

VICTOR: Ya. The nurse went and talked to him for a minute —it doesn't matter. As long as he's notified so I can go ahead.

>   *She suppresses comment, picks up a lamp.*

That's probably real porcelain. Maybe it'd go in the bedroom.

ESTHER, *putting the lamp down*: Why don't I meet you somewhere? The whole thing depresses me.

VICTOR: Why? It won't take long. Relax. Come on, sit down; the dealer'll be here any minute.

ESTHER, *sitting on a couch*: There's just something so damned rotten about it. I can't help it; it always was. The whole thing is infuriating.

VICTOR: Well, don't get worked up. We'll sell it and that'll be the end of it. I picked up the tickets, by the way.

ESTHER: Oh, good. *Laying her head back*: Boy, I hope it's a good picture.

VICTOR: Better be. Great, not good. Two-fifty apiece.

ESTHER, *with sudden protest*: I don't care! I want to go somewhere. *She aborts further response, looking around.* God, what's it all about? When I was coming up the stairs just now, and all the doors hanging open . . . It doesn't seem possible . . .

VICTOR: They tear down old buildings every day in the week, kid.

ESTHER: I know, but it makes you feel a hundred years old. I hate empty rooms. *She muses.* What was that screwball's name?—rented the front parlor, remember?—repaired saxophones?

VICTOR, *smiling*: Oh—Saltzman. *Extending his hand sideways*: With the one eye went out that way.

ESTHER: Ya! Every time I came down the stairs, there he was waiting for me with his four red hands! How'd he ever get all those beautiful girls?

VICTOR—*laughs*: God knows. He must've smelled good.

  She laughs, and he does.

He'd actually come running up here sometimes; middle of the afternoon—"Victor, come down quick, I got extras!"

ESTHER: And you did, too!

VICTOR: Why not? If it was free, you took it.

ESTHER, *blushing*: You never told me that.

VICTOR: No, that was before you. Mostly.

ESTHER: You dog.

VICTOR: So what? It was the Depression.

> *She laughs at the non sequitur.*

No, really—I think people were friendlier; lot more daytime screwing in those days. Like the McLoughlin sisters—remember, with the typing service in the front bedroom? *He laughs.* My father used to say, "In that typing service it's two dollars a copy."

> *She laughs. It subsides.*

ESTHER: And they're probably all dead.

VICTOR: I guess Saltzman would be—he was well along Although—*He shakes his head, laughs softly in surprise.* Jeeze, he wasn't either. I think he was about . . . my age now. Huh!

> *Caught by the impact of time, they stare for a moment in silence.*

ESTHER—*gets up, goes to the harp*: Well, where's your dealer?

VICTOR, *glancing at his watch*: It's twenty to six. He should be here soon.

> *She plucks the harp.*

That should be worth something.

ESTHER: I think a lot of it is. But you're going to have to bargain, you know. You can't just take what they say . . .

VICTOR, *with an edge of protest*: *I* can bargain; don't worry, I'm not giving it away.

ESTHER: Because they *expect* to bargain.

VICTOR: Don't get depressed already, will you? We didn't even start. *I* intend to bargain, I know the score with these guys.

ESTHER—*withholds further argument, goes to the phonograph; firing up some slight gaiety*: What's this record?

VICTOR: It's a Laughing Record. It was a big thing in the Twenties.

ESTHER, *curiously*: You remember it?

VICTOR: Very vaguely. I was only five or six. Used to play them at parties. You know—see who could keep a straight face. Or maybe they just sat around laughing; I don't know.

ESTHER: That's a wonderful idea!

> *Their relation is quite balanced, so to speak; he turns to her.*

VICTOR: You look good.

> *She looks at him, an embarrassed smile.*

I mean it.—I *said* I'm going to bargain, why do you . . . ?

ESTHER: I believe you.—This is the suit.

VICTOR: Oh, is that it! And how much? Turn around.

ESTHER, *turning*: Forty-five, imagine? He said nobody'd buy it, it was too simple.

VICTOR, *seizing the agreement*: Boy, women are dumb; that

is really handsome. See, I don't mind if you get something for your money, but half the stuff they sell is such crap . . . *Going to her*: By the way, look at this collar. Isn't this one of the ones you just bought?

ESTHER, *examining it*: No, that's an older one.

VICTOR: Well, even so. *Turning up a heel*: Ought to write to Consumers Union about these heels. Three weeks—look at them!

ESTHER: Well, you don't walk straight.—You're not going in uniform, I hope.

VICTOR: I could've murdered that guy! I'd just changed, and McGowan was trying to fingerprint some bum and he didn't want to be printed; so he swings out his arm just as I'm going by, right into my container.

ESTHER, *as though this symbolized*: Oh, God . . .

VICTOR: I gave it to that quick cleaner, he'll try to have it by six.

ESTHER: Was there cream and sugar in the coffee?

VICTOR: Ya.

ESTHER: He'll never have it by six.

VICTOR, *assuagingly*: He's going to try.

ESTHER: Oh, forget it.

> *Slight pause. Seriously disconsolate, she looks around at random.*

VICTOR: Well, it's only a movie . . .

ESTHER: But we go out so rarely—why must everybody know your salary? I want an evening! I want to sit down in a restaurant without some drunken ex-cop coming over to the table to talk about old times.

VICTOR: It happened twice. After all these years, Esther, it would seem to me . . .

ESTHER: I know it's unimportant—but like that man in the museum; he really did—he thought you were the sculptor.

VICTOR: So I'm a sculptor.

ESTHER, *bridling*: Well, it was nice, that's all! You really do, Vic—you look distinguished in a suit. Why not? *Laying her head back on the couch*: I should've taken down the name of that scotch.

VICTOR: All scotch is chemically the same.

ESTHER: I know; but some is better.

VICTOR, *looking at his watch*: Look at that, will you? Five-thirty sharp, he tells me. People say anything. *He moves with a heightened restlessness, trying to down his irritation with her mood. His eye falls on a partly opened drawer of a chest, and he opens it and takes out an ice skate.* Look at that, they're still good! *He tests the edge with his fingernail; she merely glances at him.* They're even sharp. We ought to skate again sometime. *He sees her unremitting moodiness.* Esther, I said I would bargain!—You see?—you don't know how to drink; it only depresses you.

ESTHER: Well, it's the kind of depression I enjoy!

VICTOR: Hot diggity dog.

ESTHER: I have an idea.

VICTOR: What?

ESTHER: Why don't you leave me? Just send me enough for coffee and cigarettes.

VICTOR: Then you'd *never* have to get out of bed.

ESTHER: I'd get out. Once in a while.

VICTOR: I got a better idea. Why don't you go off for a couple of weeks with your doctor? Seriously. It might change your viewpoint.

ESTHER: I wish I could.

VICTOR: Well, do it. He's got a suit. You could even take the dog—especially the dog. *She laughs.* It's not funny. Every time you go out for one of those walks in the rain I hold my breath what's going to come back with you.

ESTHER, *laughing*: Oh, go on, you love her.

VICTOR: I love her! You get plastered, you bring home strange animals, and I "love" them! I do not love that goddamned dog!

> She laughs with affection, as well as with a certain feminine defiance.

ESTHER: Well, I want her!

VICTOR—*pause*: It won't be solved by a dog, Esther. You're an intelligent, capable woman, and you can't lay around all day. Even something part-time, it would give you a place to go.

ESTHER: I don't need a place to go. *Slight pause.* I'm not quite used to Richard not being there, that's all.

VICTOR: He's gone, kid. He's a grown man; you've got to do something with yourself.

ESTHER: I can't go to the same place day after day. I never could and I never will. Did you *ask* to speak to your brother?

VICTOR: I asked the nurse. Yes. He couldn't break away.

ESTHER: That son of a bitch. It's sickening.

VICTOR: Well, what are you going to do? He never had that kind of feeling.

ESTHER: What feeling? To come to the phone after sixteen years? It's common decency. *With sudden intimate sympathy*: You're furious, aren't you?

VICTOR: Only at myself. Calling him again and again all week like an idiot . . . To hell with him, I'll handle it alone. It's just as well.

ESTHER: What about his share?

He shifts; pressed and annoyed.

I don't want to be a pest—but I think there could be some money here, Vic.

He is silent.

You're going to raise that with him, aren't you?

VICTOR, *with a formed decision*: I've been thinking about it. He's got a right to his half, why should he give up anything?

ESTHER: I thought you'd decided to put it to him?

VICTOR: I've changed my mind. I don't really feel he owes me anything, I can't put on an act.

ESTHER: But how many Cadillacs can he drive?

VICTOR: That's why he's got Cadillacs. People who love money don't give it away.

ESTHER: I don't know why you keep putting it like charity. There's such a thing as a moral debt. Vic, you made his whole career possible. What law said that only he could study medicine—?

VICTOR: Esther, please—let's not get back on that, will you?

ESTHER: I'm not back on anything—you were even the better student. That's a real debt, and he ought to be made to face it. He could never have finished medical school if you hadn't taken care of Pop. I mean we ought to start talking the way people talk! There could be some real money here.

VICTOR: I doubt that. There are no antiques or—

ESTHER: Just because it's ours why must it be worthless?

VICTOR: Now what's that for?

ESTHER: Because that's the way we think! We do!

VICTOR, *sharply*: The man won't even come to the phone, how am I going to—?

ESTHER: Then you write him a letter, bang on his door. This *belongs* to you!

VICTOR, *surprised, seeing how deadly earnest she is*: What are you so excited about?

ESTHER: Well, for one thing it might help you make up your mind to take your retirement.

    A slight pause.

VICTOR, *rather secretively, unwillingly*: It's not the money been stopping me.

ESTHER: Then what is it?

    He is silent.

I just thought that with a little cushion you could take a month or two until something occurs to you that you want to do.

VICTOR: It's all I think about right now, I don't have to quit to think.

ESTHER: But nothing seems to come of it.

VICTOR: Is it that easy? I'm going to be fifty. You don't just start a whole new career. I don't understand why it's so urgent all of a sudden.

ESTHER—*laughs*: All of a sudden! It's all I've been talking about since you became eligible—I've been saying the same thing for three years!

VICTOR: Well, it's not three years—

ESTHER: It'll be three years in March! It's *three years*. If you'd gone back to school then you'd almost have your Master's by now; you might have had a chance to get into something you'd love to do. Isn't that true? Why can't you make a move?

VICTOR—*pause. He is almost ashamed*: I'll tell you the truth. I'm not sure the whole thing wasn't a little unreal. I'd be fifty-three, fifty-four by the time I could start doing anything.

ESTHER: But you always knew that.

VICTOR: It's different when you're right on top of it. I'm not sure it makes any sense now.

ESTHER, *moving away, the despair in her voice*: Well . . . this is exactly what I tried to tell you a thousand times. It makes the same sense it ever made. But you might have twenty more years, and that's still a long time. Could do a lot of interesting things in that time. *Slight pause*. You're so young, Vic.

VICTOR: I am?

ESTHER: Sure! I'm not, but you are. God, all the girls goggle at you, what do you want?

VICTOR—*laughs emptily*: It's hard to discuss it, Es, because I don't understand it.

ESTHER: Well, why not talk about what you don't understand? Why do you expect yourself to be an authority?

VICTOR: Well, one of us is got to stay afloat, kid.

ESTHER: You want me to pretend everything is great? I'm bewildered and I'm going to act bewildered! *It flies out as though long suppressed*: I've asked you fifty times to write a letter to Walter—

VICTOR, *like a repeated story*: What's this with Walter again? What's Walter going to—?

ESTHER: He is an important scientist, and that hospital's building a whole new research division. I saw it in the paper, it's his hospital.

VICTOR: Esther, the man hasn't called me in sixteen years.

ESTHER: But neither have you called him!

    He looks at her in surprise.

Well, you haven't. That's also a fact.

VICTOR, *as though the idea were new and incredible*: What would I call him for?

ESTHER: Because, he's your brother, he's influential, and he could help—Yes, that's how people do, Vic! Those articles he wrote had a real idealism, there was a genuine human quality. I mean people do change, you know.

VICTOR, *turning away*: I'm sorry, I don't need Walter.

ESTHER: I'm not saying you have to approve of him; he's a

selfish bastard, but he just might be able to put you on the track of something. I don't see the humiliation.

VICTOR, *pressed, irritated*: I don't understand why it's all such an emergency.

ESTHER: Because I don't know where in hell I am, Victor! *To her own surprise, she has ended nearly screaming. He is silent. She retracts.* I'll do anything if I know why, but all these years we've been saying, once we get the pension we're going to start to live. . . . It's like pushing against a door for twenty-five years and suddenly it opens . . . and we stand there. Sometimes I wonder, maybe I misunderstood you, maybe you like the department.

VICTOR: I've hated every minute of it.

ESTHER: I did everything wrong! I swear, I think if I demanded more it would have helped you more.

VICTOR: That's not true. You've been a terrific wife—

ESTHER: I don't think so. But the security meant so much to you I tried to fit into that; but I was wrong. God—just before coming here, I looked around at the apartment to see if we could use any of this—and it's all so ugly. It's worn and shabby and tasteless. And I have good taste! I know I do! It's that everything was always temporary with us. It's like we never were anything, we were always about-to-be. I think back to the war when any idiot was making so much money—that's when you should have quit, and I knew it, I knew it!

VICTOR: That's when I wanted to quit.

ESTHER: I only had one drink, Victor, so don't—

VICTOR: Don't change the whole story, kid. I wanted to quit, and you got scared.

ESTHER: Because you said there was going to be a Depression after the war.

VICTOR: Well, go to the library, look up the papers around 1945, see what they were saying!

ESTHER: I don't care! *She turns away—from her own irrationality.*

VICTOR: I swear, Es, sometimes you make it sound like we've had no life at all.

ESTHER: God—my mother was so right! I can never believe what I see. I knew you'd never get out if you didn't during the war—I saw it happening, and I said nothing. You know what the goddamned trouble is?

VICTOR, *glancing at his watch, as he senses the end of her revolt*: What's the goddamned trouble?

ESTHER: We can never keep our minds on money! We worry about it, we talk about it, but we can't seem to *want* it. I do, but you don't. I really do, Vic. I want it. Vic? *I want money!*

VICTOR: Congratulations.

ESTHER: You go to hell!

VICTOR: I wish you'd stop comparing yourself to other people, Esther! That's all you're doing lately.

ESTHER: Well, I can't help it!

VICTOR: Then you've got to be a failure, kid, because there's always going to be somebody up ahead of you. What happened? I have a certain nature; just as you do—I didn't change—

ESTHER: But you have changed. You've been walking

around like a zombie ever since the retirement came up. You've gotten so vague—

VICTOR: Well, it's a decision. And I'd like to feel a little more certain about it. . . . Actually, I've even started to fill out the forms a couple of times.

ESTHER, *alerted*: And?

VICTOR, *with difficulty—he cannot understand it himself*: I suppose there's some kind of finality about it that . . . *He breaks off.*

ESTHER: But what else did you expect?

VICTOR: It's stupid; I admit it. But you look at that god-damned form and you can't help it. You sign your name to twenty-eight years and you ask yourself, Is that all? Is that it? And it is, of course. The trouble is, when I think of starting something new, that number comes up—five oh—and the steam goes out. But I'll do something. I will! *With a greater closeness to her now*: I don't know what it is; every-time I think about it all—it's almost frightening.

ESTHER: What?

VICTOR: Well, like when I walked in here before . . . *He looks around.* This whole thing—it hit me like some kind of craziness. Piling up all this stuff here like it was made of gold. *He half-laughs, almost embarrassed.* I brought up every stick; damn near saved the carpet tacks. *He turns to the center chair.* That whole way I was with him—it's inconceivable to me now.

ESTHER, *with regret over her sympathy*: Well . . . you loved him.

VICTOR: I know, but it's all words. What was he? A busted

businessman like thousands of others, and I acted like some kind of a mountain crashed. I tell you the truth, every now and then the whole thing is like a story somebody told me. You ever feel that way?

ESTHER: All day, every day.

VICTOR: Oh, come on—

ESTHER: It's the truth. The first time I walked up those stairs I was nineteen years old. And when you opened that box with your first uniform in it—remember that? When you put it on the first time?—how we laughed? If anything happened you said you'd call a cop! *They both laugh.* It was like a masquerade. And we were right. That's when we were right.

VICTOR, *pained by her pain*: You know, Esther, every once in a while you try to sound childish and it—

ESTHER: I mean to be! I'm sick of the— Oh, forget it, I want a drink. *She goes for her purse.*

VICTOR, *surprised*: What's that, the great adventure? Where are you going all of a sudden?

ESTHER: I can't stand it in here, I'm going for a walk.

VICTOR: Now you cut out this nonsense!

ESTHER: I am not an alcoholic!

VICTOR: You've had a good life compared to an awful lot of people! You trying to turn into a goddamned teenager or something?

ESTHER, *indicating the furniture*: Don't talk childishness to me, Victor—not in this room! You let it lay here all these years because you can't have a simple conversation with your own brother, and I'm childish? You're still eighteen years old with that man! I mean I'm stuck, but I admit it!

VICTOR, *hurt*: Okay. Go ahead.

ESTHER—*she can't quite leave*: You got a receipt? I'll get your suit. *He doesn't move. She makes it rational*: I just want to get out of here.

VICTOR—*takes out a receipt and gives it to her. His voice is cold*: It's right off Seventh. The address is on it. *He moves from her.*

ESTHER: I'm coming back right away.

VICTOR, *freeing her to her irresponsibility*: Do as you please, kid. I mean it.

ESTHER: You were grinding your teeth again last night. Did you know that?

VICTOR: Oh! No wonder my ear hurts.

ESTHER: I wish I had a tape recorder. I mean it, it's gruesome; sounds like a lot of rocks coming down a mountain. I wish you could hear it, you wouldn't take this self-sufficient attitude.

>He is silent, alarmed, hurt. He moves upstage as though looking at the furniture.

VICTOR: It's okay. I think I get the message.

ESTHER, *afraid—she tries to smile and goes back toward him*: Like what?

VICTOR—*moves a chair and does a knee bend and draws out the chassis of an immense old radio*: What other message is there?

>Slight pause.

ESTHER, *to retrieve the contact*: What's that?

VICTOR: Oh, one of my old radios that I made. Mama mia, look at those tubes.

ESTHER, *more wondering than she feels about radios*: Would that work?

VICTOR: No, you need a storage battery. . . . *Recalling, he suddenly looks up at the ceiling.*

ESTHER, *looking up*: What?

VICTOR: One of my batteries exploded, went right through there someplace. *He points.* There! See where the plaster is different?

ESTHER, *striving for some spark between them*: Is this the one you got Tokyo on?

VICTOR, *not relenting, his voice dead*: Ya, this is the monster.

ESTHER, *with a warmth*: Why don't you take it?

VICTOR: Ah, it's useless.

ESTHER: Didn't you once say you had a lab up here? Or did I dream that?

VICTOR: Sure, I took it apart when Pop and I moved up here. Walter had that wall, and I had this. We did some great tricks up here.

> *She is fastened on him.*

He avoids her eyes and moves waywardly. I'll be frank with you, kid—I look at my life and the whole thing is incomprehensible to me. I know all the reasons and all the reasons and all the reasons, and it ends up—nothing. *He goes to the harp, touches it.*

It's strange, you know? I forgot all about it—we'd work up

here all night sometimes, and it was often full of music. My mother'd play for hours down in the library. Which is peculiar, because a harp is so soft. But it penetrates, I guess.

ESTHER: You're dear. You are, Vic. *She starts toward him, but he thwarts her by looking at his watch.*

VICTOR: I'll have to call another man. Come on, let's get out of here. *With a hollow, exhausted attempt at joy:* We'll get my suit and act rich!

ESTHER: Vic, I didn't mean that I—

VICTOR: Forget it. Wait, let me put these away before somebody walks off with them. *He takes up the foil and mask.*

ESTHER: Can you still do it?

VICTOR, *his sadness, his distance clinging to him:* Oh, no, you gotta be in shape for this. It's all in the thighs—

ESTHER: Well, let me see, I never saw you do it!

VICTOR, *giving the inch:* All right, but I can't get down far enough any more. *He takes position, feet at right angles, bouncing himself down to a difficult crouch.*

ESTHER: Maybe you could take it up again.

VICTOR: Oh no, it's a lot of work, it's the toughest sport there is. *Resuming position:* Okay, just stand there.

ESTHER: Me?

VICTOR: Don't be afraid. *Snapping the tip:* It's a beautiful foil, see how alive it is? I beat Princeton with this. *He laughs tiredly and makes a tramping lunge from yards away; the button touches her stomach.*

ESTHER, *springing back:* God! Victor!

VICTOR: What?

ESTHER: You looked beautiful.

He laughs, surprised and half-embarrassed—when both of them are turned to the door by a loud, sustained coughing out in the corridor. The coughing increases.

Enter Gregory Solomon. In brief, a phenomenon; a man nearly ninety but still straight-backed and the air of his massiveness still with him. He has perfected a way of leaning on his cane without appearing weak.

He wears a worn fur-felt black fedora, its brim turned down on the right side like Jimmy Walker's —although much dustier—and a shapeless topcoat. His frayed tie has a thick knot, askew under a curled-up collar tab. His vest is wrinkled, his trousers baggy. A large diamond ring is on his left index finger. Tucked under his arm, a wrung-out leather portfolio. He hasn't shaved today.

Still coughing, catching his breath, trying to brush his cigar ashes off his lapel in a hopeless attempt at businesslike decorum, he is nodding at Esther and Victor and has one hand raised in a promise to speak quite soon. Nor has he failed to glance with some suspicion at the foil in Victor's hand.

VICTOR: Can I get you a glass of water?

Solomon gestures an imperious negative, trying to stop coughing.

ESTHER: Why don't you sit down?

Solomon gestures thanks, sits in the center armchair, the cough subsiding.

You sure you don't want some water?

SOLOMON, *in a Russian-Yiddish accent*: Water I don't need; a little blood I could use. Thank you. *He takes deep breaths, his attention on Victor, who now puts down the foil.* Oh boy. That's some stairs.

ESTHER: You all right now?

SOLOMON: Another couple steps you'll be in heaven. Ah—excuse me, Officer, I am looking for a party. The name is . . . *He fingers in his vest.*

VICTOR: Franz.

SOLOMON: That's it, Franz.

VICTOR: That's me.

> *Solomon looks incredulous.*

Victor Franz.

SOLOMON: So it's a policeman!

VICTOR, *grinning*: Uh huh.

SOLOMON: What do you know! *Including Esther*: You see? There's only one beauty to this lousy business, you meet all kinda people. But I never dealt with a policeman. *Reaching over to shake hands*: I'm very happy to meet you. My name is Solomon, Gregory Solomon.

VICTOR, *shaking hands*: This is my wife.

ESTHER: How do you do.

SOLOMON, *nodding appreciatively to Esther*: Very nice. *To Victor*: That's a nice-looking woman. *He extends his hands to her.* How do you do, darling. Beautiful suit.

ESTHER—*laughs*: The fact is, I just bought it!

SOLOMON: You got good taste. Congratulations, wear it in good health. *He lets go her hand.*

ESTHER: I'll go to the cleaner, dear. I'll be back soon. *With a step toward the door—to Solomon*: Will you be very long?

SOLOMON, *glancing around at the furniture as at an antagonist*: With furniture you never know, can be short, can be long, can be medium.

ESTHER: Well, you give him a good price now, you hear?

SOLOMON: Ah ha! *Waving her out*: Look, you go to the cleaner, and we'll take care everything one hundred per cent.

ESTHER: Because there's some very beautiful stuff here. I know it, but he doesn't.

SOLOMON: I'm not sixty-two years in the business by taking advantage. Go, enjoy the cleaner.

She and Victor laugh.

ESTHER, *shaking her finger at him*: I hope I'm going to like you!

SOLOMON: Sweetheart, all the girls like me, what can I do?

ESTHER, *still smiling—to Victor as she goes to the door*: You be careful.

VICTOR, *nodding*: See you later.

She goes.

SOLOMON: I like her, she's suspicious.

VICTOR, *laughing in surprise*: What do you mean by that?

SOLOMON: Well, a girl who believes everything, how you gonna trust her?

Victor laughs appreciatively.

I had a wife . . . *He breaks off with a wave of the hand.* Well, what's the difference? Tell me, if you don't mind, how did you get my name?

VICTOR: In the phone book.

SOLOMON: You don't say! The phone book.

VICTOR: Why?

SOLOMON, *cryptically*: No-no, that's fine, that's fine.

VICTOR: The ad said you're a registered appraiser.

SOLOMON: Oh yes. I am registered, I am licensed, I am even vaccinated.

Victor laughs.

Don't laugh, the only thing you can do today without a license is you'll go up the elevator and jump out the window. But I don't have to tell you, you're a policeman, you know this world. *Hoping for contact*: I'm right?

VICTOR, *reserved*: I suppose.

SOLOMON, *surveying the furniture, one hand on his thigh, the other on the chair arm in a naturally elegant position*: So. *He glances about again, and with an uncertain smile*: That's a lot of furniture. This is all for sale?

VICTOR: Well, ya.

SOLOMON: Fine, fine. I just like to be sure where we are. *With a weak attempt at a charming laugh*: Frankly, in this neighborhood I never expected such a load. It's very surprising.

VICTOR: But I said it was a whole houseful.

SOLOMON, *with a leaven of unsureness*: Look, don't worry about it, we'll handle everything very nice. *He gets up from the chair and goes to one of the pair of chiffoniers which he is obviously impressed with. He looks up at the chandeliers. Then straight at Victor*: I'm not mixing in, Officer, but if you wouldn't mind—what is your connection? How do you come to this?

VICTOR: It was my family.

SOLOMON: You don't say. Looks like it's standing here a long time, no?

VICTOR: Well, the old man moved everything up here after the '29 crash. My uncles took over the house and they let him keep this floor.

SOLOMON, *as though to emphasize that he believes it*: I see. *He walks to the harp.*

VICTOR: Can you give me an estimate now, or do you have to—?

SOLOMON, *running a hand over the harp frame*: No-no, I'll give you right away, I don't waste a minute, I'm very busy. *He plucks a string, listens. Then bends down and runs a hand over the sounding board*: He passed away, your father?

VICTOR: Oh, long time ago—about sixteen years.

SOLOMON, *standing erect*: It's standing here sixteen years?

VICTOR: Well, we never got around to doing anything about it, but they're tearing the building down, so . . . It was very good stuff, you know—they had quite a little money.

SOLOMON: Very good, yes . . . I can see. *He leaves the harp with an estimating glance.* I was also very good; now I'm not so good. Time, you know, is a terrible thing. *He is a distance from the harp and indicates it.* That sounding board is cracked, you know. But don't worry about it, it's still a nice object. *He goes to an armoire and strokes the veneer.* It's a funny thing—an armoire like this, thirty years you couldn't give it away; it was a regular measles. Today all of a sudden, they want it again. Go figure it out. *He goes to one of the chests.*

VICTOR, *pleased*: Well, give me a good price and we'll make a deal.

SOLOMON. Definitely. You see, I don't lie to you. *He is pointing to the chest.* For instance, a chiffonier like this I wouldn't have to keep it a week. *Indicating the other chest*: That's a pair, you know.

VICTOR: I know.

SOLOMON: That's a nice chairs, too. *He sits on a dining-room chair, rocking to test its tightness.* I like the chairs.

VICTOR: There's more stuff in the bedroom, if you want to look.

SOLOMON: Oh? *He goes toward the bedroom.* What've you got here? *He looks into the bedroom, up and down.* I like the bed. That's a very nice carved bed. That I can sell. That's your parents' bed?

VICTOR: Yes. They may have bought that in Europe, if I'm not mistaken. They used to travel a good deal.

SOLOMON: Very handsome, very nice. I like it. *He starts to return to the center chair, eyes roving the furniture.* Looks a very nice family.

VICTOR: By the way, that dining-room table opens up. Probably seat about twelve people.

SOLOMON, *looking at the table*: I know that. Yes. In a pinch even fourteen. *He picks up the foil.* What's this? I thought you were stabbing your wife when I came in.

VICTOR, *laughing*: No, I just found it. I used to fence years ago.

SOLOMON: You went to college?

VICTOR: Couple of years, ya.

SOLOMON: That's very interesting.

VICTOR: It's the old story.

SOLOMON: No, listen—What happens to people is always the main element to me. Because when do they call me? It's either a divorce or somebody died. So it's always a new story. I mean it's the same, but it's different. *He sits in the center chair.*

VICTOR: You pick up the pieces.

SOLOMON: That's very good, yes. I pick up the pieces. It's a little bit like you, I suppose. You must have some stories, I betcha.

VICTOR: Not very often.

SOLOMON: What are you, a traffic cop, or something . . . ?

VICTOR: I'm out in Rockaway most of the time, the airports.

SOLOMON: That's Siberia, no?

VICTOR, *laughing*: I like it better that way.

SOLOMON: You keep your nose clean.

VICTOR, *smiling*: That's it. *Indicating the furniture*: So what do you say?

SOLOMON: What I say? *Taking out two cigars as he glances about*: You like a cigar?

VICTOR: Thanks, I gave it up long time ago.

VICTOR: So what's the story here?

SOLOMON: I can see you are a very factual person.

VICTOR: You hit it.

SOLOMON: Couldn't be better. So tell me, you got some kind of paper here? To show ownership?

VICTOR: Well, no, I don't. But . . . *He half-laughs*. I'm the owner, that's all.

SOLOMON: In other words, there's no brothers, no sisters.

VICTOR: I have a brother, yes.

SOLOMON: Ah hah. You're friendly with him. Not that I'm mixing in, but I don't have to tell you the average family they love each other like crazy, but the minute the parents die is all of a sudden a question who is going to get what and you're covered with cats and dogs—

VICTOR: There's no such problem here.

SOLOMON: Unless we're gonna talk about a few pieces, then it wouldn't bother me, but to take the whole load without a paper is a—

VICTOR: All right, I'll get you some kind of statement from him; don't worry about it.

SOLOMON: That's definite; because even from high-class people you wouldn't believe the shenanigans—lawyers, college professors, television personalities—five hundred dollars they'll pay a lawyer to fight over a bookcase it's worth fifty cents—because you see, everybody wants to be number one, so . . .

VICTOR: I said I'd get you a statement. *He indicates the room.* Now what's the story?

SOLOMON: All right, so I'll tell you the story. *He looks at the dining-room table and points to it.* For instance, you mention the dining-room table. That's what they call Spanish Jacobean. Cost maybe twelve, thirteen hundred dollars. I would say—1921, '22. I'm right?

VICTOR: Probably, ya.

SOLOMON—*clears his throat*: I see you're an intelligent man, so before I'll say another word, I ask you to remember—with used furniture you cannot be emotional.

VICTOR—*laughs*: I haven't opened my mouth!

SOLOMON: I mean you're a policeman, I'm a furniture dealer, we both know this world. Anything Spanish Jacobean you'll sell quicker a case of tuberculosis.

VICTOR: Why? That table's in beautiful condition.

SOLOMON: Officer, you're talking reality; you cannot talk reality with used furniture. They don't like that style; not only they don't like it, they hate it. The same thing with that buffet there and that . . . *He starts to point elsewhere.*

VICTOR: You only want to take a few pieces, is that the ticket?

SOLOMON: Please, Officer, we're already talking too fast—

VICTOR: No-no, you're not going to walk off with the gravy and leave me with the bones. All or nothing or let's forget it. I told you on the phone it was a whole houseful.

SOLOMON: What're you in such a hurry? Talk a little bit, we'll see what happens. In a day they didn't build Rome. *He calculates worriedly for a moment, glancing again at the pieces he wants. He gets up, goes and touches the harp.* You see, what I had in mind—I would give you such a knockout price for these few pieces that you—

VICTOR: That's *out*.

SOLOMON, *quickly*: Out.

VICTOR: I'm not running a department store. They're tearing the building down.

SOLOMON: Couldn't be better! We understand each other, so—*with his charm*—so there's no reason to be emotional. *He goes to the records.* These records go? *He picks up one.*

VICTOR: I might keep three or four.

SOLOMON, *reading a label*: Look at that! Gallagher and Shean!

VICTOR, *with only half a laugh*: You're not going to start playing them now!

SOLOMON: Who needs to play? I was on the same bill with Gallagher and Shean maybe fifty theaters.

VICTOR, *surprised*: You were an actor?

SOLOMON: An actor! An acrobat; my whole family was acrobats. *Expanding with this first opening*: You never heard "The Five Solomons"—may they rest in peace? I was the one on the bottom.

VICTOR: Funny—I never heard of a Jewish acrobat.

SOLOMON: What's the matter with Jacob, he wasn't a wrestler?—wrestled with the Angel?

Victor laughs.

Jews been acrobats since the beginning of the world. I was a horse them days: drink, women, anything—on-the-go, on-the-go, nothing ever stopped me. Only life. Yes, my boy. *Almost lovingly putting down the record*: What do you know, Gallagher and Shean.

VICTOR, *more intimately now, despite himself; but with no less persistence in keeping to the business*: So where are we?

SOLOMON—*glancing off, he turns back to Victor with a deeply concerned look*: Tell me, what's with crime now? It's up, hey?

VICTOR: Yeah, it's up, it's up. Look, Mr. Solomon, let me make one thing clear, heh? I'm not sociable.

SOLOMON: You're not.

VICTOR: No, I'm not; I'm not a businessman, I'm not good at conversations. So let's get to a price, and finish. Okay?

SOLOMON: You don't want we should be buddies.

VICTOR: That's exactly it.

SOLOMON: So we wouldn't be buddies! *He sighs.* But just so you'll know me a little better—I'm going to show you something. *He takes out a leather folder which he flips open and hands to Victor.* There's my discharge from the British Navy. You see? "His Majesty's Service."

VICTOR, *looking at the document*: Huh! What were you doing in the British Navy?

SOLOMON: Forget the British Navy. What does it say the date of birth?

VICTOR: "Eighteen . . ." *Amazed, he looks up at Solomon.* You're almost ninety?

SOLOMON: Yes, my boy. I left Russia sixty-five years ago, I was twenty-four years old. And I smoked all my life. I drinked, and I loved every woman who would let me. So what do I need to steal from you?

VICTOR: Since when do people need a reason to steal?

SOLOMON: I never saw such a man in my life!

VICTOR: Oh yes you did. Now you going to give me a figure or—?

SOLOMON—*he is actually frightened because he can't get a hook into Victor and fears losing the good pieces*: How can I give you a figure? You don't trust one word I say!

VICTOR, *with a strained laugh*: I never saw you before, what're you asking me to trust you?!

SOLOMON, *with a gesture of disgust*: But how am I going to start to talk to you? I'm sorry; here you can't be a policeman. If you want to do business a little bit you gotta believe or you can't do it. I'm . . . I'm . . . Look, forget it. *He gets up and goes to his portfolio.*

VICTOR, *astonished*: What are you doing?

SOLOMON: I can't work this way. I'm too old every time I open my mouth you should practically call me a thief.

VICTOR: Who called you a thief?

SOLOMON, *moving toward the door*: No—I don't need it. I don't want it in my shop. *Wagging a finger into Victor's face*: And don't forget it—I never gave you a price, and look what you did to me. You see? I never gave you a price!

VICTOR, *angering*: Well, what did you come here for, to do me a favor? What are you talking about?

SOLOMON: Mister, I pity you! What is the matter with you people! You're worse than my daughter! Nothing in the world you believe, nothing you respect—how can you live? You think that's such a smart thing? That's so hard, what you're doing? Let me give you a piece advice—it's not that you can't believe nothing, that's not so hard—it's that you still got to believe it. *That's* hard. And if you can't do that, my friend—you're a dead man! *He starts toward the door.*

VICTOR, *chastened despite himself*: Oh, Solomon, come on, will you?

SOLOMON: No-no. You got a certain problem with this furniture but you don't want to listen so how can I talk?

VICTOR: I'm listening! For Christ's sake, what do you want me to do, get down on my knees?

SOLOMON, *putting down his portfolio and taking out a wrinkled tape measure from his jacket pocket*: Okay, come here. I realize you are a factual person, but some facts are funny. *He stretches the tape measure across the depth of a piece.* What does that read? *Then turns to Victor, showing him.*

VICTOR—*comes to him, reads*: Forty inches. So?

SOLOMON: My boy, the bedroom doors in a modern apartment house are thirty, thirty-two inches maximum. So you can't get this in—

VICTOR: What about the old houses?

SOLOMON, *with a desperation growing*: All I'm trying to tell you is that my possibilities are smaller!

VICTOR: Well, can't I ask a question?

SOLOMON: I'm giving you architectural facts! Listen—*Wiping his face, he seizes on the library table, going to it.* You got there, for instance, a library table. That's a solid beauty. But go find me a modern apartment with a library. If they would build old hotels, I could sell this, but they only build new hotels. People don't live like this no more. This stuff is from another world. So I'm trying to give you a modern viewpoint. Because the price of used furniture is nothing but a viewpoint, and if you wouldn't understand the viewpoint is impossible to understand the price.

VICTOR: So what's the viewpoint—that it's all worth nothing?

SOLOMON: That's what you said, I didn't say that. The chairs is worth something, the chiffoniers, the bed, the harp—

VICTOR—*turns away from him*: Okay, let's forget it, I'm not giving you the cream—

SOLOMON: What're you jumping!

VICTOR, *turning to him*: Good God, are you going to make me an offer or not?

SOLOMON; *walking away with a hand at his temple*: Boy, oh boy, oh boy. You must've arrested a million people by now.

VICTOR: Nineteen in twenty-eight years.

SOLOMON: So what are you so hard on me?

VICTOR: Because you talk about everything but money and I don't know what the hell you're up to.

SOLOMON, *raising a finger*: We will now talk money. *He returns to the center chair.*

VICTOR: Great. I mean you can't blame me—every time you open your mouth the price seems to go down.

SOLOMON, *sitting*: My boy, the price didn't change since I walked in.

VICTOR, *laughing*: That's even better! So what's the price?

> *Solomon glances about, his wit failed, a sunk look coming over his face.*

What's going on? What's bothering you?

SOLOMON: I'm sorry, I shouldn't have come. I thought it would be a few pieces but . . . *Sunk, he presses his fingers into his eyes.* It's too much for me.

VICTOR: Well, what'd you come for? I told you it was the whole house.

SOLOMON, *protesting*: You called me so I came! What should I do, lay down and die? *Striving again to save it*: Look, I want very much to make you an offer, the only question is . . . *He breaks off as though fearful of saying something.*

VICTOR: This is a hell of a note.

SOLOMON: Listen, it's a terrible temptation to me! But . . . *As though throwing himself on Victor's understanding*: You see, I'll tell you the truth; you must have looked in a very old phone book; a couple of years ago already I cleaned out my store. Except a few English andirons I got left, I sell when I need a few dollars. I figured I was eighty, eighty-five, it was time already. But I waited—and nothing happened—I even moved out of my apartment. I'm living in the back of the store with a hotplate. But nothing happened. I'm still practically a hundred per cent—not a hundred, but I feel very well. And I figured maybe you got a couple nice pieces—not that the rest can't be sold, but it could take a year, year and half. For me that's a big bet. *In conflict, he looks around.* The trouble is I love to work; I love it, but— *Giving up*: I don't know what to tell you.

VICTOR: All right, let's forget it then.

SOLOMON, *standing*: What're you jumping?

VICTOR: Well, are you in or out!

SOLOMON: How do I know where I am! You see, it's also this particular furniture—the average person he'll take one look, it'll make him very nervous.

VICTOR: Solomon, you're starting again.

SOLOMON: I'm not bargaining with you!

VICTOR: Why'll it make him nervous?

SOLOMON: Because he knows it's never gonna break.

VICTOR, *not in bad humor, but clinging to his senses*: Oh come on, will you? Have a little mercy.

SOLOMON: My boy, you don't know the psychology! If it wouldn't break there is no more possibilities. For instance, you take—*crosses to table*—this table . . . Listen! *He bangs the table.* You can't move it. A man sits down to such a table he knows not only he's married, he's got to stay married— there is no more possibilities.

    Victor laughs.

You're laughing, I'm telling you the factual situation. What is the key word today? Disposable. The more you can throw it away the more it's beautiful. The car, the furniture, the wife, the children—everything has to be disposable. Because you see the main thing today is—shopping. Years ago a person, he was unhappy, didn't know what to do with himself—he'd go to church, start a revolution—*something*. Today you're unhappy? Can't figure it out? What is the salvation? Go shopping.

VICTOR, *laughing*: You're terrific, I have to give you credit.

SOLOMON: I'm telling you the truth! If they would close the stores for six months in this country there would be from coast to coast a regular massacre. With this kind of furniture the shopping is over, it's finished, there's no more possibilities, you *got* it, you see? So you got a problem here.

VICTOR, *laughing*: Solomon, you are one of the greatest. But I'm way ahead of you, it's not going to work.

SOLOMON, *offended*: What "work"? I don't know how much time I got. What is so terrible if I say that? The trouble is, you're such a young fella you don't understand these things—

VICTOR: I understand very well, I know what you're up against. I'm not so young.

SOLOMON, *scoffing*: What are you, forty? Forty-five?

VICTOR: I'm going to be fifty.

SOLOMON: Fifty! You're a baby boy!

VICTOR: Some baby.

SOLOMON: My God, if I was fifty . . . ! I got married I was seventy-five.

VICTOR: Go on.

SOLOMON: What are you talking? She's still living by

Eighth Avenue over there. See, that's why I like to stay
liquid, because I don't want her to get her hands on this. . . .
Birds she loves. She's living there with maybe a hundred
birds. She gives you a plate of soup it's got feathers. I didn't
work all my life for them birds

VICTOR: I appreciate your problems, Mr. Solomon, but I
don't have to pay for them. *He stands.* I've got no more time.

SOLOMON, *holding up a restraining hand—desperately*: I'm
going to buy it! *He has shocked himself, and glances around
at the towering masses of furniture.* I mean I'll . . . *He
moves, looking at the stuff.* I'll have to live, that's all, I'll
make up my mind! I'll buy it.

VICTOR—*he is affected as Solomon's fear comes through to
him*: We're talking about everything now.

SOLOMON, *angrily*: Everything, everything! *Going to his
portfolio*: I'll figure it up, I'll give you a very nice price,
and you'll be a happy man.

VICTOR, *sitting again*: That I doubt.

   Solomon takes a hard-boiled egg out of the portfolio.

What's this now, lunch?

SOLOMON: You give me such an argument, I'm hungry! I'm
not supposed to get too hungry.

VICTOR: Brother!

SOLOMON—*cracks the shell on his diamond ring*: You want
me to starve to death? I'm going to be very quick here.

VICTOR: Boy—I picked a number!

SOLOMON: There wouldn't be a little salt, I suppose.

VICTOR: I'm not going running for salt now!

SOLOMON: Please, don't be blue. I'm going to knock you off your feet with the price, you'll see. *He swallows the egg. He now faces the furniture, and, half to himself, pad and pencil poised*: I'm going to go here like an IBM. *He starts estimating on his pad.*

VICTOR: That's all right, take it easy. As long as you're serious.

SOLOMON: Thank you. *He touches the hated buffet*: Ay, yi, yi. All right, well . . . *He jots down a figure. He goes to the next piece, jots down another figure. He goes to another piece, jots down a figure.*

VICTOR, *after a moment*: You really got married at seventy-five?

SOLOMON: What's so terrible?

VICTOR: No, I think it's terrific. But what was the point?

SOLOMON: What's the point at twenty-five? You can't die twenty-six?

VICTOR, *laughing softly*: I guess so, ya.

SOLOMON: It's the same like secondhand furniture, you see; the whole thing is a viewpoint. It's a mental world. *He jots down another figure for another piece.* Seventy-five I got married, fifty-one, and twenty-two.

VICTOR: You're kidding.

SOLOMON: I wish! *He works, jotting his estimate of each piece on the pad, opening drawers, touching everything. Peering into a dark recess, he takes out a pencil flashlight, switches it on, and begins to probe with the beam.*

VICTOR—*he has gradually turned to watch Solomon, who goes on working*: Cut the kidding now—how old are you?

SOLOMON, *sliding out a drawer*: I'm eighty-nine. It's such an accomplishment?

VICTOR: You're a hell of a guy.

SOLOMON, *smiling with the encouragement and turning to Victor*: You know, it's a funny thing. It's so long since I took on such a load like this—you forget what kind of life it puts into you. To take out a pencil again . . . it's a regular injection. Frankly, my telephone you could use for a ladle, it wouldn't interfere with nothing. I want to thank you. *He points at Victor.* I'm going to take good care of you, I mean it. I can open that?

VICTOR: Sure, anything.

SOLOMON, *going to an armoire*: Some of them had a mirror . . . *He opens the armoire, and a rolled-up fur rug falls out. It is about three by five.* What's this?

VICTOR: God knows. I guess it's a rug.

SOLOMON, *holding it up*: No-no—that's a lap robe. Like for a car.

VICTOR: Say, that's right, ya. When they went driving. God, I haven't seen that in—

SOLOMON: You had a chauffeur?

VICTOR: Ya, we had a chauffeur.

> *Their eyes meet. Solomon looks at him as though Victor were coming into focus. Victor turns away. Now Solomon turns back to the armoire.*

SOLOMON: Look at that! *He takes down an opera hat from the shelf within.* My God! *He puts it on, looks into the interior mirror.* What a world! *He turns to Victor*: He must've been some sporty guy!

VICTOR, *smiling*: You look pretty good!

SOLOMON: And from all this he could go so broke?

VICTOR: Why not? Sure. Took five weeks. Less.

SOLOMON: You don't say. And he couldn't make a come-back?

VICTOR: Well some men don't bounce, you know.

SOLOMON—*grunts*: Hmm! So what did he do?

VICTOR: Nothing. Just sat here. Listened to the radio.

SOLOMON: But what did he do? What—?

VICTOR: Well, now and then he was making change at the Automat. Toward the end he was delivering telegrams.

SOLOMON, *with grief and wonder*: You don't say. And how much he had?

VICTOR: Oh . . . couple of million, I guess.

SOLOMON: My God. What was the matter with him?

VICTOR: Well, my mother died around the same time. I guess that didn't help. Some men just don't bounce, that's all.

SOLOMON: Listen, I can tell you bounces. I went busted 1932; then 1923 they also knocked me out; the panic of 1904, 1898 . . . But to lay down like *that* . . .

VICTOR: Well, you're different. He believed in it.

SOLOMON. What he believed?

VICTOR: The system, the whole thing. He thought it was his fault, I guess. You—you come in with your song and dance, it's all a gag. You're a hundred and fifty years old, you tell your jokes, people fall in love with you, and you walk away with their furniture.

SOLOMON: That's not nice.

VICTOR: Don't shame me, will ya?—What do you say? You don't need to look any more, you know what I've got here.

> Solomon is clearly at the end of his delaying resources. He looks about slowly; the furniture seems to loom over him like a threat or a promise. His eyes climb up to the edges of the ceiling, his hands grasping one another.

What are you afraid of? It'll keep you busy.

> Solomon looks at him, wanting even more reassurance.

SOLOMON: You don't think it's foolish?

VICTOR: Who knows what's foolish? You enjoy it—

SOLOMON: Listen, I love it—

VICTOR:—so take it. You plan too much, you end up with nothing.

SOLOMON, *intimately*: I would like to tell you something. The last few months, I don't know what it is—she comes to me. You see, I had a daughter, she should rest in peace, she took her own life, a suicide. . . .

VICTOR: When was this?

SOLOMON: It was . . . 1916—the latter part. But very beautiful, a lovely face, with large eyes—she was pure like the morning. And lately, I don't know what it is—I see her

clear like I see you. And every night practically, I lay down
to go to sleep, so she sits there. And you can't help it, you
ask yourself—what happened? What *happened*? Maybe I
could have said something to her . . . maybe I *did* say something . . . it's all . . . *He looks at the furniture.* It's not that
I'll die, you can't be afraid of that. But . . . I'll tell you the
truth—a minute ago I mentioned I had three wives . . .
Slight pause. His fear rises. Just this minute I realize I had
four. Isn't that terrible? The first time was nineteen, in
Lithuania. See, that's what I mean—it's impossible to know
what is important. Here I'm sitting with you . . . and . . .
and . . . *He looks around at the furniture.* What for? Not
that I don't want it, I want it, but . . . You see, all my life
I was a terrible fighter—you could never take nothing from
me; I pushed, I pulled, I struggled in six different countries,
I nearly got killed a couple times, and it's . . . It's like now
I'm sitting here talking to you and I tell you it's a dream,
it's a dream! You see, you can't imagine it because—

VICTOR: I know what you're talking about. But it's not a
dream—it's that you've got to make decisions before you
know what's involved, but you're stuck with the results anyway. Like I was very good in science—I loved it. But I had
to drop out to feed the old man. And I figured I'd go on
the Force temporarily, just to get us through the Depression,
then go back to school. But the war came, we had the kid,
and you turn around and you've racked up fifteen years on
the pension. And what you started out to do is a million
miles away. Not that I regret it all—we brought up a terrific
boy, for one thing; nobody's ever going to take that guy.
But it's like you were saying—it's impossible to know what's
important. We always agreed, we stay out of the rat race
and live our own life. That was important. But you shovel

the crap out the window, it comes back in under the door—
it all ends up she wants, she wants. And I can't really blame
her—there's just no respect for anything but money.

SOLOMON: What're you got against money?

VICTOR: Nothing, I just didn't want to lay down my life for
it. But I think I laid it down another way, and I'm not even
sure any more what I was trying to accomplish. I look back
now, and all I can see is a long, brainless walk in the street.
I guess it's the old story; do anything, but just be sure you
win. Like my brother; years ago I was living up here with
the old man, and he used to contribute five dollars a month.
A *month!* And a successful surgeon. But the few times he'd
come around, the expression on the old man's face—you'd
think God walked in. The respect, you know what I mean?
The respect! And why not? Why not?

SOLOMON: Well, sure, he had the power.

VICTOR: Now you said it—if you got that you got it all.
You're even lovable! *He laughs.* Well, what do you say? Give
me the price.

SOLOMON—*slight pause*: I'll give you eleven hundred dollars.

VICTOR—*slight pause*: For everything?

SOLOMON, *in a breathless way*: Everything.

> *Slight pause. Victor looks around at the furniture.*

I want it so I'm giving you a good price. Believe me, you
will never do better. I want it; I made up my mind.

> *Victor continues staring at the stuff. Solomon takes
> out a common envelope and removes a wad of bills.*

Here . . . I'll pay you now. *He readies a bill to start counting
it out.*

VICTOR: It's that I have to split it, see—

SOLOMON: All right . . . so I'll make out a receipt for you and I'll put down six hundred dollars.

VICTOR: No-no . . . *He gets up and moves at random, looking at the furniture.*

SOLOMON: Why not? He took from you so take from him. If you want, I'll put down four hundred.

VICTOR: No, I don't want to do that. *Slight pause.* I'll call you tomorrow.

SOLOMON, *smiling*: All right; with God's help if I'm there tomorrow I'll answer the phone. If I wouldn't be . . . *Slight pause.* Then I wouldn't be.

VICTOR, *annoyed, but wanting to believe*: Don't start that again, will you?

SOLOMON: Look, you convinced me, so I want it. So what should I do?

VICTOR: *I* convinced *you*?

SOLOMON, *very distressed*: Absolutely you convinced me. You saw it—the minute I looked at it I was going to walk out!

VICTOR, *cutting him off, angered at his own indecision*: Ah, the hell with it. *He holds out his hand.* Give it to me.

SOLOMON, *wanting Victor's good will*: Please, don't be blue.

VICTOR: Oh, it all stinks. *Jabbing forth his hand*: Come on.

SOLOMON, *with a bill raised over Victor's hand—protesting*: What stinks? You should be happy. Now you can buy her a nice coat, take her to Florida, maybe—

VICTOR, *nodding ironically*: Right, right! We'll all be happy now. Give it to me.

> *Solomon shakes his head and counts bills into his hand. Victor turns his head and looks at the piled walls of furniture.*

SOLOMON: There's one hundred; two hundred; three hundred; four hundred . . . Take my advice, buy her a nice fur coat your troubles'll be over—

VICTOR: I know all about it. Come on.

SOLOMON: So you got there four, so I'm giving you . . . five, six, seven . . . I mean it's already in the Bible, the rat race. The minute she laid her hand on the apple, that's it.

VICTOR: I never read the Bible. Come on.

SOLOMON: If you'll read it you'll see—there's always a rat race, you can't stay out of it. So you got there seven, so now I'm giving you . . .

> *A man appears in the doorway. In his mid-fifties, well-barbered; hatless, in a camel's-hair coat, very healthy complexion. A look of sharp intelligence on his face.*
> *Victor, seeing past Solomon, starts slightly with shock, withdrawing his hand from the next bill which Solomon is about to lay in it.*

VICTOR, *suddenly flushed, his voice oddly high and boyish*: Walter!

WALTER—*enters the room, coming to Victor with extended hand and with a reserve of warmth but a stiff smile*: How are you, kid?

> *Solomon has moved out of their line of sight.*

VICTOR—*shifts the money to his left hand as he shakes*: God, I never expected you.

WALTER, *of the money—half-humorously*: Sorry I'm late. What are you doing?

VICTOR, *fighting a treason to himself, thus taking on a strained humorous air*: I . . . I just sold it.

WALTER: Good! How much?

VICTOR, *as though absolutely certain now he has been had*: Ah . . . eleven hundred.

WALTER, *in a dead voice shorn of comment*: Oh. Well, good. *He turns rather deliberately—but not overly so—to Solomon*: For everything?

SOLOMON—*comes to Walter, his hand extended; with an energized voice that braves everything*: I'm very happy to meet you, Doctor! My name is Gregory Solomon.

WALTER—*the look on his face is rather amused, but his reserve has possibilities of accusation*: How do you do?
> *He shakes Solomon's hand, as Victor raises his hand to smooth down his hair, a look of near-alarm for himself on his face.*

CURTAIN

Act Two

The action is continuous. As the curtain rises Walter is just releasing Solomon's hand and turning about to face Victor. His posture is reserved, stiffened by traditional control over a nearly fierce curiosity. His grin is disciplined and rather hard, but his eyes are warm and combative.

WALTER: How's Esther?

VICTOR: Fine. Should be here any minute.

WALTER: Here? Good! And what's Richard doing?

VICTOR: He's at M.I.T.

WALTER: No kidding! M.I.T.!

VICTOR, *nodding*: They gave him a full scholarship.

WALTER, *dispelling his surprise*: What do you know. *With a wider smile, and embarrassed warmth*: You're proud.

VICTOR: I guess so. They put him in the Honors Program.

WALTER: Really. That's wonderful.—You don't mind my coming, do you?

VICTOR: No! I called you a couple of times.

WALTER: Yes, my nurse told me. What's Richard interested in?

53

VICTOR: Science. So far, anyway. *With security*: How're yours?

WALTER—*moving, he breaks the confrontation*: I suppose Jean turned out best—but I don't think you ever saw her.

VICTOR: I never did, no.

WALTER: The *Times* gave her quite a spread last fall. Pretty fair designer.

VICTOR: Oh? That's great. And the boys? They in school?

WALTER: They often are. *Abruptly laughs, refusing his own embarrassment*: I hardly see them, Vic. With all the unsolved mysteries in the world they're investigating the guitar. But what the hell . . . I've given up worrying about them. *He walks past Solomon, glancing at the furniture*: I'd forgotten how much he had up here. There's your radio!

VICTOR, *smiling with him*: I know, I saw it.

WALTER, *looking down at the radio, then upward to the ceiling through which the battery once exploded. Both laugh. Then he glances with open feeling at Victor*: Long time.

VICTOR, *fending off the common emotion*: Yes. How's Dorothy?

WALTER, *cryptically*: She's all right, I guess. *He moves, glancing at the things, but again with suddenness turns back.* Looking forward to seeing Esther again. She still writing poetry?

VICTOR: No, not for years now.

SOLOMON: He's got a very nice wife. We met.

WALTER, *surprised; as though at something intrusive*: Oh? *He turns back to the furniture.* Well. Same old junk, isn't it?

VICTOR, *downing a greater protest*: I wouldn't say that. Some of it isn't bad.

SOLOMON: One or two very nice things, Doctor. We came to a very nice agreement.

VICTOR, *with an implied rebuke*: I never thought you'd show up; I guess we'd better start all over again—

WALTER: Oh, no-no, I don't want to foul up your deal.

SOLOMON: Excuse me, Doctor—better you should take what you want now than we'll argue later. What did you want?

WALTER, *surprised, turning to Victor*: Oh, I didn't want anything. I came by to say hello, that's all.

VICTOR: I see. *Fending off Walter's apparent gesture with an over-quick movement toward the oar*: I found your oar, if you want it.

WALTER: Oar?

> *Victor draws it out from behind furniture. A curved-blade sweep.*

Hah! *He receives the oar, looks up its length, and laughs, hefting it.* I must have been out of my mind!

SOLOMON: Excuse me, Doctor; if you want the oar—

WALTER, *standing the oar before Solomon, whom he leaves holding on to it*: Don't get excited, I don't want it.

SOLOMON: No. I was going to say—a personal thing like this I have no objection.

WALTER, *half-laughing*: That's very generous of you.

VICTOR, *apologizing for Solomon*: I threw in everything— I never thought you'd get here.

WALTER, *with a strained over-agreeableness*: Sure, that's all right. What are you taking?

VICTOR: Nothing, really. Esther might want a lamp or something like that.

SOLOMON: He's not interested, you see; he's a modern person, what are you going to do?

WALTER: You're not taking the harp?

VICTOR, *with a certain guilt*: Well, nobody plays . . . You take it, if you like.

SOLOMON: You'll excuse me, Doctor—the harp, please, that's another story . . .

WALTER—*laughs*—*archly amused and put out*: You don't mind if I make a suggestion, do you?

SOLOMON: Doctor, please, don't be offended, I only—

WALTER: Well, why do you interrupt? Relax, we're only talking. We haven't seen each other for a long time.

SOLOMON: Couldn't be better; I'm very sorry. *He sits, nervously pulling his cheek.*

WALTER, *touching the harp*: Kind of a pity—this was Grandpa's wedding present, you know.

VICTOR, *looking with surprise at the harp*: Say—that's right!

WALTER, *to Solomon*: What are you giving him for this?

SOLOMON: I didn't itemize—one price for everything. Maybe three hundred dollars. That sounding board is cracked, you know.

VICTOR, *to Walter*: You want it?

1) Jeffrey DeMunn as Victor Franz and Lizbeth Mackay as Esther Franz in the 1999 Broadway production of *The Price*.

2) Jeffrey DeMunn (*left*) as Victor Franz and Bob Dishy as Gregory Solomon.

3) Harris Yulin (*left*) as Walter Franz and Jeffrey DeMunn as Victor Franz.

4) The cast of the 1999 Broadway production of *The Price*. From left to right: Bob Dishy as Gregory Solomon, Jeffrey DeMunn as Victor Franz, Harris Yulin as Walter Franz and Lizbeth Mackay as Esther Franz. All photographs of the 1999 Broadway production by Richard Feldman.

SOLOMON: Please, Victor, I hope you're not going to take that away from me. *To Walter*: Look, Doctor, I'm not trying to fool you. The harp is the heart and soul of the deal. I realize it was your mother's harp, but like I tried to tell— *to Victor*—you before—*to Walter*—with used furniture you cannot be emotional.

WALTER: I guess it doesn't matter. *To Victor*: Actually, I was wondering if he kept any of Mother's evening gowns, did he?

VICTOR: I haven't really gone through it all—

SOLOMON, *raising a finger, eagerly*: Wait, wait, I think I can help you. *He goes to an armoire he had earlier looked into, and opens it.*

WALTER, *moving toward the armoire*: She had some spectacular—

SOLOMON, *drawing out the bottom of a gown elaborately embroidered in gold*: Is this what you mean?

WALTER: Yes, that's the stuff!

> *Solomon blows dust off and hands him the bottom of the gown.*

Isn't that beautiful! Say, I think she wore this at my wedding! *He takes it out of the closet, holds it up.* Sure! You remember this?

VICTOR: What do you want with it?

WALTER, *drawing out another gown off the rack*: Look at this one! Isn't that something? I thought Jeannie might make something new out of the material, I'd like her to wear something of Mother's.

VICTOR—*a new, surprising idea*: Oh! Fine, that's a nice idea.

SOLOMON: Take, take—they're beautiful.

WALTER, *suddenly glancing about as he lays the gowns across a chair*: What happened to the piano?

VICTOR: Oh, we sold that while I was still in school. We lived on it for a long time.

WALTER, *very interestedly*: I never knew that.

VICTOR: Sure. And the silver.

WALTER: Of course! Stupid of me not to remember that. *He half-sits against the back of a couch. His interest is avid, and his energy immense.* I suppose you know—you've gotten to look a great deal like Dad.

VICTOR: *I* do?

WALTER: It's very striking. And your voice is very much like his.

VICTOR: I know. It has that sound to me, sometimes.

SOLOMON: So, gentlemen . . . *He moves the money in his hand.*

VICTOR, *indicating Solomon*: Maybe we'd better settle this now.

WALTER: Yes, go ahead! *He walks off, looking at the furniture.*

SOLOMON, *indicating the money Victor holds*: You got there seven—

WALTER, *oblivious of Solomon; unable, so to speak, to settle for the status quo*: Wonderful to see you looking so well.

VICTOR—*the new interruption seems odd; observing more than speaking*: You do too, you look great.

WALTER: I ski a lot; and I ride nearly every morning. . . You know, I started to call you a dozen times this year—*He breaks off. Indicating Solomon*: Finish up, I'll talk to you later.

SOLOMON: So now I'm going to give you—*A bill is poised over Victor's hand.*

VICTOR, *to Walter*: That price all right with you?

WALTER: Oh, I don't want to interfere. It's just that I dealt with these fellows when I split up Dorothy's and my stuff last year, and I found—

VICTOR, *from an earlier impression*: You're not divorced, are you?

WALTER, *with a nervous shot of laughter*: Yes!

> *Esther enters on his line; she is carrying a suit in a plastic wrapper.*

ESTHER, *surprised*: Walter! For heaven's sake!

WALTER, *eagerly jumping up, coming to her, shaking her hand*: How are you, Esther!

ESTHER, *between her disapproval and fascinated surprise*: What are *you* doing here?

WALTER: You've hardly changed!

ESTHER, *with a charged laugh, conflicted with herself*: Oh, go on now! *She hangs the suit on a chest handle.*

WALTER, *to Victor*: You son of a gun, she looks twenty-five!

VICTOR, *watching for Esther's reaction*: I know!

ESTHER, *flattered, and offended, too*: Oh stop it, Walter! *She sits.*

WALTER: But you do, honestly; you look marvelous.

SOLOMON: It's that suit, you see? What did I tell you, it's a very beautiful suit.

> Victor laughs a little as Esther looks conflicted by Solomon's compliment.

ESTHER, *with mock-affront—to Victor*: What are you laughing at? It is. *She is about to laugh.*

VICTOR: You looked so surprised, that's all.

ESTHER: Well, I'm not used to walking into all these compliments! *She bursts out laughing.*

WALTER, *suddenly recalling—eagerly*: Say! I'm sorry I didn't know I'd be seeing you when I left the house this morning—I'd have brought you some lovely Indian bracelets. I got a whole boxful from Bombay.

ESTHER, *still not focused on Walter, sizing him up*: How do you come to—?

WALTER: I operated on this big textile guy and he keeps sending me things. He sent me this coat, in fact.

ESTHER: I was noticing it. That's gorgeous material.

WALTER: Isn't it? Two gallstones.

ESTHER, *her impression lingering for the instant*: How's Dorothy?—Did I hear you saying you were—?

WALTER, *very seriously*: We're divorced, ya. Last winter.

ESTHER: I'm sorry to hear that.

WALTER: It was coming a long time. We're both much better off—we're almost friendly now. *He laughs.*

ESTHER: Oh, stop that, you dog.

WALTER, *with naïve excitement*: It's true!

ESTHER: Look, I'm for the woman, so don't hand me that. *To Victor—seeing the money in his hand*: Have you settled everything?

VICTOR: Just about, I guess.

WALTER: I was just telling Victor—*to Victor*: when we split things up I—*to Solomon*: you ever hear of Spitzer and Fox?

SOLOMON: Thirty years I know Spitzer and Fox. Bert Fox worked for me maybe ten, twelve years.

WALTER: They did my appraisal.

SOLOMON: They're good boys. Spitzer is not as good as Fox, but between the two you're in good hands.

WALTER: Yes. That's why I—

SOLOMON: Spitzer is vice president of the Appraisers' Association.

WALTER: I see. The point I'm making—

SOLOMON: I used to be president.

WALTER: Really.

SOLOMON: Oh yes. I made it all ethical.

WALTER, *trying to keep a straight face—and Victor as well*: Did you?

Victor suddenly bursts out laughing, which sets off Walter and Esther, and a warmth springs up among them.

SOLOMON, *smiling, but insistent*: What's so funny? Listen, before me was a jungle—you wouldn't laugh so much. I put in all the rates, what we charge, you know—I made it a profession, like doctors, lawyers—used to be it was a regular snakepit. But today, you got nothing to worry—all the members are hundred per cent ethical.

WALTER: Well, that was a good deed, Mr. Solomon—but I think you can do a little better on this furniture.

ESTHER, *to Victor, who has money in his hand*: How much has he offered?

VICTOR, *embarrassed, but braving it quite well*: Eleven hundred.

ESTHER, *distressed; with a transcendent protest*: Oh, I think that's . . . isn't that very low? *She looks to Walter's confirmation.*

WALTER, *familiarly*: Come on, Solomon. He's been risking his life for you every day; be generous—

SOLOMON, *to Esther*: That's a real brother! Wonderful. *To Walter*: But you can call anybody you like—Spitzer and Fox, Joe Brody, Paul Cavallo, Morris White—I know them all and I know what they'll tell you.

VICTOR, *striving to retain some assurance; to Esther*: See, the point he was making about it—

SOLOMON, *to Esther, raising his finger*: Listen to him because he—

VICTOR, *to Solomon*: Hold it one second, will you? *To*

Esther and Walter: Not that I'm saying it's true, but he claims a lot of it is too big to get into the new apartments.

ESTHER, *half-laughing*: You believe that?

WALTER: I don't know, Esther, Spitzer and Fox said the same thing.

ESTHER: Walter, the city is full of big, old apartments!

SOLOMON: Darling, why don't you leave it to the boys?

ESTHER, *suppressing an outburst*: I wish you wouldn't order me around, Mr. Solomon! *To Walter, protesting*: Those two bureaus alone are worth a couple of hundred dollars!

WALTER, *delicately*: Maybe I oughtn't interfere—

ESTHER: Why? *Of Solomon*: Don't let him bulldoze you—

SOLOMON: My dear girl, you're talking without a basis—

ESTHER, *slashing*: I don't like this kind of dealing, Mr. Solomon! I just don't like it! *She is near tears. A pause. She turns back to Walter*: This money is very important to us, Walter.

WALTER, *chastised*: Yes. I . . . I'm sorry, Esther. *He looks about.* Well . . . if it was mine—

ESTHER: Why? It's yours as much as Victor's.

WALTER: Oh no, dear—I wouldn't take anything from this.

> *Pause.*

VICTOR: No, Walter, you get half.

WALTER: I wouldn't think of it, kid. I came by to say hello, that's all.

> *Pause.*

ESTHER—*she is very moved*: That's terrific, Walter. It's . . . Really, I . . .

VICTOR: Well, we'll talk about it.

WALTER: No-no, Vic, you've earned it. It's yours.

VICTOR, *rejecting the implication*: Why have I earned it? You take your share.

WALTER: Why don't we discuss it later? *To Solomon*: In my opinion—

SOLOMON, *to Victor*: So now you don't even have to split. *To Victor and Walter*: You're lucky they're tearing the building down—you got together, finally.

WALTER: I would have said a minimum of three thousand dollars.

ESTHER: That's exactly what I had in mind! *To Solomon*: I was going to say thirty-five hundred dollars.

WALTER, *to Victor; tactfully*: In that neighborhood.

> *Silence. Solomon sits there holding back comment, not looking at Victor, blinking with protest. Victor thinks for a moment; then turns to Solomon, and there is a wide discouragement in his voice.*

VICTOR: Well? What do you say?

SOLOMON, *spreading out his hands helplessly, outraged*: What can I say? It's ridiculous. Why does he give you three thousand? What's the matter with five thousand, ten thousand?

WALTER, *to Victor, without criticism*: You should've gotten a couple of other estimates, you see, that's always the—

VICTOR: I've been calling you all week for just that reason, Walter, and you never came to the phone.

WALTER, *blushing*: Why would that stop you from—?

VICTOR: I didn't think I had the right to do it alone—the nurse gave you my messages, didn't she?

WALTER: I've been terribly tied up—and I had no intention of taking anything for myself, so I assumed—

VICTOR: But how was I supposed to know that?

WALTER, *with open self-reproach*: Yes. Well, I . . . I beg your pardon. *He decides to stop there.*

SOLOMON: Excuse me, Doctor, but I can't understand you; first it's a lot of junk—

ESTHER: Nobody called it a lot of junk!

SOLOMON: He called it a lot of junk, Esther, when he walked in here.

    Esther turns to Walter, puzzled and angry.

WALTER, *reacting to her look; to Solomon*: Now just a minute—

SOLOMON: No, please. *Indicating Victor*: This is a factual man, so let's be factual.

ESTHER: Well, that's an awfully strange thing to say, Walter.

WALTER, *intimately*: I didn't mean it in that sense, Esther—

SOLOMON: Doctor, please. You said junk.

WALTER, *sharply—and there is an over-meaning of much greater anger in his tone*: I didn't mean it in that sense, Mr. Solomon! *He controls himself—and, half to Esther*: When you've been brought up with things, you tend to be sick of them. . . . *To Esther*: That's all I meant.

SOLOMON: My dear man, if it was Louis Seize, Biedermeier, something like that, you wouldn't get sick.

WALTER, *pointing to a piece, and weakened by knowing he is exaggerating*: Well, there happens to be a piece right over there in Biedermeier style!

SOLOMON: Biedermeier "style!" *He picks up his hat.* I got a hat it's in Borsolino style but it's not a Borsolino. *To Victor*: I mean he don't have to charge me to make an impression.

WALTER, *striving for an air of amusement*: Now what's that supposed to mean?

VICTOR, *with a refusal to dump Solomon*: Well, what basis *do* you go on, Walter?

WALTER, *reddening but smiling*: I don't know . . . it's a feeling, that's all.

ESTHER—*there is ridicule*: Well, on what basis do you take eleven hundred, dear?

VICTOR, *angered; his manly leadership is suddenly in front*: I simply felt it was probably more or less right!

ESTHER, *as a refrain*: Oh God, here we go again. All right, throw it away—

SOLOMON, *indicating Victor*: Please, Esther, he's not throwing nothing away. This man is no fool! *To Walter as well*: Excuse me, but this is not right to do to him!

WALTER, *bridling, but retaining his smile*: You going to teach me what's right now?

ESTHER, *to Victor, expanding Walter's protest*: Really! I mean.

VICTOR—*obeying her protest for want of a certainty of his own, he touches Solomon's shoulder*: Mr. Solomon . . . why don't you sit down in the bedroom for a few minutes and let us talk?

SOLOMON: Certainly, whatever you say. *He gets up.* Only please, you made a very nice deal, you got no right to be ashamed. . . . *To Esther*: Excuse me, I don't want to be personal.

ESTHER—*laughs angrily*: He's fantastic!

VICTOR, *trying to get him moving again*: Whyn't you go inside?

SOLOMON: I'm going; I only want you to understand, Victor, that if it was a different kind of man—*turning to Esther*: I would say to you that he's got the money in his hand, so the deal is concluded.

WALTER: He can't conclude any deal without me, Solomon, I'm half owner here.

SOLOMON, *to Victor*: You see? What did I ask you the first thing I walked in here? "Who is the owner?"

WALTER: Why do you confuse everything? I'm not making any claim, I merely—

SOLOMON: Then how do you come to interfere? He's got the money; I know the law!

WALTER, *angering*: Now you stop being foolish! Just stop it! I've got the best lawyers in New York, so go inside and sit down.

VICTOR, *as he turns back to escort Solomon*: Take it easy, Walter, come on, cut it out.

ESTHER, *striving to keep a light, amused tone*: Why? He's perfectly right.

VICTOR, *with a hard glance at her, moving upstage with Solomon*: Here, you better hold onto this money.

SOLOMON: No, that's yours; you hold . . .

> *He sways. Victor grasps his arm. Walter gets up.*

WALTER: You all right?

SOLOMON—*dizzy, he grasps his head*: Yes, yes, I'm . . .

WALTER, *coming to him*: Let me look at you. *He takes Solomon's wrists, looks into his face.*

SOLOMON: I'm only a little tired, I didn't take my nap today.

WALTER: Come in here, lie down for a moment. *He starts Solomon toward the bedroom.*

SOLOMON: Don't worry about me, I'm . . . *He halts and points back at his portfolio, leaning on a chest.* Please, Doctor, if you wouldn't mind—I got a Hershey's in there.

> *Walter hesitates to do his errand.*

Helps me.

> *Walter unwillingly goes to the portfolio and reaches into it.*

I'm a very healthy person, but a nap, you see, I have to have a . . .

> *Walter takes out an orange.*

Not the orange—on the bottom is a Hershey's.

> *Walter takes out a Hershey bar.*

That's a boy.

WALTER—*returns to him and helps him to the bedroom*: All right, come on . . . easy does it . . .

SOLOMON, *as he goes into the bedroom*: I'm all right, don't worry. You're very nice people.

> *Solomon and Walter exit into the bedroom. Victor glances at the money in his hand, then puts it on a table, setting the foil on it.*

ESTHER: Why are you being so apologetic?

VICTOR: About what?

ESTHER: That old man. Was that his first offer?

VICTOR: Why do you believe Walter? He was obviously pulling a number out of a hat.

ESTHER: Well, I agree with him. Did you try to get him to go higher?

VICTOR: I don't know how to bargain and I'm not going to start now.

ESTHER: I wish you wouldn't be above everything, Victor, we're not twenty years old. We need this money.

> *He is silent.*

You hear me?

VICTOR: I've made a deal, and that's it. You know, you take a tone sometimes—like I'm some kind of an incompetent.

ESTHER—*gets up, moves restlessly*: Well anyway, you'll get the whole amount.—God, he's certainly changed. It's amazing.

VICTOR, *without assent*: Seems so, ya.

ESTHER, *wanting him to join her*: He's so human! And he laughs!

VICTOR: I've seen him laugh.

ESTHER, *with a grin of trepidation*: Am I hearing something or is that my imagination?

VICTOR: I want to think about it.

ESTHER, *quietly*: You're not taking his share?

VICTOR: I said I would like to think . . .

> *Assuming he will refuse Walter's share, she really doesn't know what to do or where to move, so she goes for her purse with a quick stride.*

VICTOR, *getting up*: Where you going?

ESTHER, *turning back on him*: I want to know. Are you or aren't you taking his share?

VICTOR: Esther, I've been calling him all week; doesn't even bother to come to the phone, walks in here and smiles and I'm supposed to fall into his arms? I can't behave as though nothing ever happened, and you're not going to either! Now just take it easy, we're not dying of hunger.

ESTHER: I don't understand what you think you're upholding!

VICTOR, *outraged*: Where have you been?!

ESTHER: But he's doing exactly what you thought he should do! What do you *want*?

VICTOR: Certain things have happened, haven't they? I can't turn around this fast, kid. He's only been here ten minutes, I've got twenty-eight years to shake off my back. . . . Now sit down, I want you here. *He sits.*

She remains standing, uncertain of what to do.

Please. You can wait a few minutes for your drink.

ESTHER, *in despair*: Vic, it's all blowing away.

VICTOR, *to diminish the entire prize*: Half of eleven hundred dollars is five-fifty, dear.

ESTHER: I'm not talking about money.

Voices are heard from the bedroom.

He's obviously making a gesture, why can't you open yourself a little? *She lays her head back.* My mother was right— I can never believe anything I see. But I'm going to. That's all I'm going to do. What I see.

A chair scrapes in the bedroom.

VICTOR: Wipe your cheek, will you?

Walter enters from the bedroom.

How is he?

WALTER: I think he'll be all right. *Warmly*: God, what a pirate! *He sits.* He's eighty-nine!

ESTHER: I don't believe it!

VICTOR: He is. He showed me his—

WALTER, *laughing*: Oh, he show you that too?

VICTOR, *smiling*: Ya, the British Navy.

ESTHER: *He* was in the British Navy?

VICTOR, *building on Walter's support*: He's got a discharge. He's not altogether phony.

WALTER: I wouldn't go that far. A guy that age, though,

still driving like that . . . *As though admitting Victor was not foolish*: There *is* something wonderful about it.

VICTOR, *understating*: *I* think so.

ESTHER: What do you think we ought to do, Walter?

WALTER—*slight pause. He is trying to modify what he believes is his overpowering force so as not to appear to be taking over. He is faintly smiling toward Victor*: There is a way to get a good deal more out of it. I suppose you know that, though.

VICTOR: Look, I'm not married to this guy. If you want to call another dealer we can compare.

WALTER: You don't have to do that; he's a registered appraiser.—You see, instead of selling it, you could make it a charitable contribution.

VICTOR: I don't understand.

WALTER: It's perfectly simple. He puts a value on it—let's say twenty-five thousand dollars, and—

ESTHER, *fascinated with a laugh*: Are you kidding?

WALTER: It's done all the time. It's a dream world but it's legal. He estimates its highest retail value, which could be put at some such figure. Then I donate it to the Salvation Army. I'd have to take ownership, you see, because my tax rate is much higher than yours so it would make more sense if I took the deduction. I pay around fifty per cent tax, so if I make a twenty-five-thousand-dollar contribution I'd be saving around twelve thousand in taxes. Which we could split however you wanted to. Let's say we split it in half, I'd give you six thousand dollars. *A pause.* It's really the only sensible way to do it, Vic.

ESTHER—*glances at Victor, but he remains silent*: Would it be costing you anything?

WALTER: On the contrary—it's found money to me. *To Victor*: I mentioned it to him just now.

VICTOR, *as though this had been the question*: What'd he say?

WALTER: It's up to you. We'd pay him an appraisal fee—fifty, sixty bucks.

VICTOR: Is he willing to do that?

WALTER: Well, of course he'd rather buy it outright, but what the hell—

ESTHER: Well, that's not his decision, is it?

VICTOR: No . . . it's just that I feel I did come to an agreement with him and I—

WALTER: Personally, I wouldn't let that bother me. He'd be making fifty bucks for filling out a piece of paper.

ESTHER: That's not bad for an afternoon.

  Pause.

VICTOR: I'd like to think about it.

ESTHER: There's not much time, though, if you want to deal with *him*.

VICTOR, *cornered*: I'd like a few minutes, that's all.

WALTER, *to Esther*: Sure . . . let him think it over. *To Victor*: It's perfectly legal, if that's what's bothering you. I almost did it with my stuff but I finally decided to keep it. *He laughs*. In fact, my own apartment is so loaded up it doesn't look too different from this.

ESTHER: Well, maybe you'll get married again.

WALTER: I doubt that very much, Esther.—I often feel I never should have.

ESTHER, *scoffing*: Why!

WALTER: Seriously. I'm in a strange business, you know. There's too much to learn and far too little time to learn it. And there's a price you have to pay for that. I tried awfully hard to kid myself but there's simply no time for people. Not the way a woman expects, if she's any kind of woman. *He laughs*. But I'm doing pretty well alone!

VICTOR: How would I list an amount like that on my income tax?

WALTER: Well . . . call it a gift.

> *Victor is silent, obviously in conflict. Walter sees the emotion.*

Not that it is, but you could list it as such. It's allowed.

VICTOR: I see. I was just curious how it—

WALTER: Just enter it as a gift. There's no problem.

> *With the first sting of a vague resentment, Walter turns his eyes away. Esther raises her eyebrows, staring at the floor. Walter lifts the foil off the table —clearly changing the subject.*

You still fence?

VICTOR, *almost gratefully pursuing this diversion*: No, you got to join a club and all that. And I work weekends often. I just found it here.

WALTER, *as though to warm the mood*: Mother used to love to watch him do this.

ESTHER, *surprised, pleased*: Really?

WALTER: Sure, she used to come to all his matches.

ESTHER, *to Victor, somehow charmed*: You never told me that.

WALTER: Of course; she's the one made him take it up. *He laughs to Victor.* She thought it was elegant!

VICTOR: Hey, that's right!

WALTER, *laughing at the memory*: He did look pretty good too! *He spreads his jacket away from his chest.* I've still got the wounds! *To Victor, who laughs*: Especially with those French gauntlets she—

VICTOR, *recalling*: Say . . .! *Looking around with an enlivened need*: I wonder where the hell . . . *He suddenly moves toward a bureau.* Wait, I think they used to be in . . .

ESTHER, *to Walter*: *French* gauntlets?

WALTER: She brought them from Paris. Gorgeously embroidered. He looked like one of the musketeers.

> *Out of the drawer where he earlier found the ice skate, Victor takes a pair of emblazoned gauntlets.*

VICTOR: Here they are! What do you know!

ESTHER, *reaching her hand out*: Aren't they beautiful!

> *He hands her one.*

VICTOR: God, I'd forgotten all about them. *He slips one on his hand.*

WALTER: Christmas, 1929.

VICTOR, *moving his hand in the gauntlet*: Look at that, they're still soft . . . *To Walter—a little shy in asking*: How do you remember all this stuff?

WALTER: Why not? Don't you?

ESTHER: He doesn't remember your mother very well.

VICTOR: I remember her. *Looking at the gauntlet*: It's just her face; somehow I can never *see* her.

WALTER, *warmly*: That's amazing, Vic. *To Esther*: She adored him.

ESTHER, *pleased*: Did she?

WALTER: Victor? If it started to rain she'd run all the way to school with his galoshes. Her Victor—my God! By the time he could light a match he was already Louis Pasteur.

VICTOR: It's odd . . . like the harp! I can almost hear the music . . . But I can never see her face. Somehow. *For a moment, silence, as he looks across at the harp.*

WALTER: What's the problem?

> *Pause. Victor's eyes are swollen with feeling. He turns and looks up at Walter, who suddenly is embarrassed and oddly anxious.*

SOLOMON—*enters from the bedroom. He looks quite distressed. He is in his vest, his tie is open. Without coming downstage*: Please, Doctor, if you wouldn't mind I would like to . . . *He breaks off, indicating the bedroom.*

WALTER: What is it?

SOLOMON: Just for one minute, please.

Walter stands. Solomon glances at Victor and Esther and returns to the bedroom.

WALTER: I'll be right back. *He goes rather quickly up and into the bedroom.*

A pause. Victor is sitting in silence, unable to face her.

ESTHER, *with delicacy and pity, sensing his conflicting feelings*: Why can't you take him as he is?

He glances at her.

Well you can't expect him to go into an apology, Vic—he probably sees it all differently, anyway.

He is silent. She comes to him.

I know it's difficult, but he is trying to make a gesture, I think.

VICTOR: I guess he is, yes.

ESTHER: You know what would be lovely? If we could take a few weeks and go to like . . . out-of-the-way places . . . just to really break it up and see all the things that people do. You've been around such mean, petty people for so long and little ugly tricks. I'm serious—it's not romantic. We're much too suspicious of everything.

VICTOR, *staring ahead*: Strange guy.

ESTHER: Why?

VICTOR: Well, to walk in that way—as though nothing ever happened.

ESTHER: Why not? What can be done about it?

VICTOR—*slight pause*: I feel I have to say something.

ESTHER, *with a slight trepidation, less than she feels*: What can you say?

VICTOR: You feel I ought to just take the money and shut up, heh?

ESTHER: But what's the point of going backwards?

VICTOR, *with a self-bracing tension*: I'm not going to take this money unless I talk to him.

ESTHER, *frightened*: You can't bear the thought that he's decent.

> *He looks at her sharply.*

That's all it is, dear. I'm sorry, I have to say it.

VICTOR, *without raising his voice*: I can't bear that he's *decent*!

ESTHER: You throw this away, you've got to explain it to me. You can't go on blaming everything on him or the system or God knows what else! You're free and you can't make a move, Victor, and that's what's driving me crazy! *Silence. Quietly*: Now take this money.

> *He is silent, staring at her.*

You take this money! Or I'm washed up. You hear me? If you're stuck it doesn't mean I have to be. Now that's it.

> *Movements are heard within the bedroom. She straightens. Victor smooths down his hair with a slow, preparatory motion of his hand, like one adjusting himself for combat.*

WALTER—*enters from the bedroom, smiling, shaking his head. Indicating the bedroom*: Boy—we got a tiger here. What is this between you, did you know him before?

VICTOR: No. Why? What'd he say?

WALTER: He's still trying to buy it outright. *He laughs.* He talks like you added five years by calling him up.

VICTOR: Well, what's the difference, I don't mind.

WALTER, *registering the distant rebuke*: No, that's fine, that's all right. *He sits. Slight pause.* We don't understand each other, do we?

VICTOR, *with a certain thrust, matching Walter's smile*: I am a little confused, Walter . . . yes.

WALTER: Why is that?

> *Victor doesn't answer at once.*

Come on, we'll all be dead soon!

VICTOR: All right, I'll give you one example. When I called you Monday and Tuesday and again this morning—

WALTER: I've explained that.

VICTOR: But I don't make phone calls to pass the time. Your nurse sounded like I was a pest of some kind . . . it was humiliating.

WALTER—*oddly, he is over-upset*: I'm terribly sorry, she shouldn't have done that.

VICTOR: I know, Walter, but I can't imagine she takes that tone all by herself.

WALTER, *aware now of the depth of resentment in Victor*:

Oh no—she's often that way. I've never referred to you like that.

Victor is silent, not convinced.

Believe me, will you? I'm terribly sorry. I'm overwhelmed with work, that's all it is.

VICTOR: Well, you asked me, so I'm telling you.

WALTER: Yes! You should! But don't misinterpret that. *Slight pause. His tension has increased. He braves a smile.* Now about this tax thing. He'd be willing to make the appraisal twenty-five thousand. *With difficulty*: If you'd like, I'd be perfectly willing for you to have the whole amount I'd be saving.

Slight pause.

ESTHER: Twelve thousand?

WALTER: Whatever it comes to.

Pause. Esther slowly looks to Victor.

You must be near retirement now, aren't you?

ESTHER, *excitedly*: He's past it. But he's trying to decide what to do.

WALTER: Oh. *To Victor—near open embarrassment now*: It would come in handy, then, wouldn't it?

Victor glances at him as a substitute for a reply.

I don't need it, that's all, Vic. Actually, I've been about to call you for quite some time now.

VICTOR: What for?

WALTER—*suddenly, with a strange quick laugh, he reaches and touches Victor's knee*: Don't be suspicious!

VICTOR, *grinning*: I'm just trying to figure it out, Walter.

WALTER: Yes, good. All right. *Slight pause.* I thought it was time we got to know one another. That's all.

Slight pause.

VICTOR: You know, Walter, I tried to call you a couple of times before this about the furniture—must be three years ago.

WALTER: I was sick.

VICTOR, *surprised*: Oh . . . Because I left a lot of messages.

WALTER: I was quite sick. I was hospitalized.

ESTHER: What happened?

WALTER—*slight pause. As though he were not quite sure whether to say it*: I broke down.

Slight pause.

VICTOR: I had no idea.

WALTER: Actually, I'm only beginning to catch up with things. I was out of commission for nearly three years. *With a thrust of success*: But I'm almost thankful for it now— I've never been happier!

ESTHER: You seem altogether different!

WALTER: I think I am, Esther. I live differently, I think differently. All I have now is a small apartment. And I got rid of the nursing homes—

VICTOR: What nursing homes?

WALTER, *with a removed self-amusement*: Oh, I owned three nursing homes. There's big money in the aged, you know.

Helpless, desperate children trying to dump their parents—
nothing like it. I even pulled out of the market. Fifty per
cent of my time now is in City hospitals. And I tell you, I'm
alive. For the first time. I do medicine, and that's it. *Attempting an intimate grin*: Not that I don't soak the rich
occasionally, but only enough to live, really. *It is as though
this was his mission here, and he waits for Victor's comment.*

VICTOR: Well, that must be great.

WALTER, *seizing on this minute encouragement*: Vic, I wish
we could talk for weeks, there's so much I want to tell
you. . . . *It is not rolling quite the way he would wish and he
must pick examples of his new feelings out of the air.* I never
had friends—you probably know that. But I do now, I
have good friends. *He moves, sitting nearer Victor, his
enthusiasm flowing.* It all happens so gradually. You start
out wanting to be the best, and there's no question that you
do need a certain fanaticism; there's so much to know and so
little time. Until you've eliminated everything extraneous—
he smiles—including people. And of course the time comes
when you realize that you haven't merely been specializing in
something—something has been specializing in you. You
become a kind of instrument, an instrument that cuts money
out of people, or fame out of the world. And it finally makes
you stupid. Power can do that. You get to think that because
you can frighten people they love you. Even that you love
them.—And the whole thing comes down to fear. One night
I found myself in the middle of my living room, dead drunk
with a knife in my hand, getting ready to kill my wife.

ESTHER: Good Lord!

WALTER: Oh ya—and I nearly made it too! *He laughs.*
But there's one virtue in going nuts—provided you survive,

of course. You get to see the terror—not the screaming kind, but the slow, daily fear you call ambition, and cautiousness, and piling up the money. And really, what I wanted to tell you for some time now—is that you helped me to understand that in myself.

VICTOR: Me?

WALTER: Yes. *He grins warmly, embarrassed.* Because of what you did. I could never understand it, Vic—after all, you *were* the better student. And to stay with a job like that through all those years seemed . . . *He breaks off momentarily, the uncertainty of Victor's reception widening his smile.* You see, it never dawned on me until I got sick—that you'd made a choice.

VICTOR: A choice, how?

WALTER: You wanted a real life. And that's an expensive thing; it costs. *He has found his theme now; sees he has at last touched something in Victor. A breath of confidence comes through now.* I know I may sound terribly naïve, but I'm still used to talking about anything that matters. Frankly, I didn't answer your calls this week because I was afraid. I've struggled so long for a concept of myself and I'm not sure I can make it believable to you. But I'd like to. *He sees permission to go on in Victor's perplexed eyes*: You see, I got to a certain point where . . . I dreaded my own work; I finally couldn't cut. There are times, as you know, when if you leave someone alone he might live a year or two; while if you go in you might kill him. And the decision is often . . . not quite, but almost . . . arbitrary. But the odds are acceptable, provided you think the right thoughts. Or don't think at all, which I managed to do till then. *Slight pause. He is no longer smiling; instead, a near-embarrassment is on him.* I ran into a cluster of misjudgments. It can happen, but it never had to me, not one on top of the other. And they had one thing in common; they'd all been diagnosed by other men as inoperable. And quite suddenly the . . . the whole prospect of my own motives opened up. Why had I taken risks that very competent men had declined? And the quick answer, of course, is—to pull off the impossible. Shame the competition. But suddenly I saw something else. And it was terror. In dead center, directing my brains, my hands, my ambition—for thirty years.

> *Slight pause.*

VICTOR: Terror of what?

> *Pause.*

WALTER, *his gaze direct on Victor now*: Of it ever happening to me—*he glances at the center chair*—as it happened to him. Overnight, for no reason, to find yourself degraded and thrown-down. *With the faintest hint of impatience and challenge*: You know what I'm talking about, don't you?

> *Victor turns away slightly, refusing commitment.*

Isn't that why you turned your back on it all?

VICTOR, *sensing the relevancy to himself now*: Partly. Not altogether, though.

WALTER: Vic, we were both running from the same thing. I thought I wanted to be tops, but what it was was untouchable. I ended in a swamp of success and bankbooks, you on civil service. The difference is that you haven't hurt other people to defend yourself. And I've learned to respect that, Vic; you simply tried to make yourself useful.

ESTHER: That's wonderful—to come to such an understand-stand with yourself.

WALTER: Esther, it's a strange thing; in the hospital, for the first time since we were boys, I began to feel . . . like a brother. In the sense that we shared something. *To Victor*: And I feel I would know how to be friends now.

VICTOR—*slight pause; he is unsure*: Well fine. I'm glad of that.

WALTER—*sees the reserve but feels he has made headway and presses on a bit more urgently*: You see, that's why you're still so married. That's a very rare thing. And why your boy's in such good shape. You've lived a real life. *To Esther*: But you know that better than I.

ESTHER: I don't know what I know, Walter.

WALTER: Don't doubt it, dear—believe me, you're fortunate people. *To Victor*: You know that, don't you?

VICTOR, *without looking at Esther*: I think so.

ESTHER: It's not quite as easy as you make it, Walter.

WALTER—*hesitates, then throws himself into it*: Look, I've had a wild idea—it'll probably seem absurd to you, but I wish you'd think about it before you dismiss it. I gather you haven't decided what to do with yourself now? You're re-tiring . . . ?

VICTOR: I'll decide one of these days, I'm still thinking.

WALTER, *nervously*: Could I suggest something?

VICTOR: Sure, go ahead.

WALTER: We've been interviewing people for the new wing. For the administrative side. Kind of liaison people between the scientists and the board. And it occurred to me several times that you might fit in there.

> *Slight pause.*

ESTHER, *with a release of expectation*: That would be wonderful!

VICTOR—*slight pause. He glances at her with suppression, but his voice betrays excitement*: What could I do there, though?

WALTER, *sensing Victor's interest*: It's kind of fluid at the moment, but there's a place for people with a certain amount of science who—

VICTOR: I have no degree, you know.

WALTER: But you've had analytic chemistry, and a lot of math and physics, if I recall. If you thought you needed it you could take some courses in the evenings. I think you have enough background.—How would you feel about that?

VICTOR, *digging in against the temptation*: Well . . . I'd like to know more about it, sure.

ESTHER, *as though to press him to accept*: It'd be great if he could work in science, it's really the only thing he ever wanted.

WALTER: I know; it's a pity he never went on with it. *Turning to Victor*: It'd be perfectly simple, Vic, I'm chairman of the committee. I could set it all up—

> *Solomon enters. They turn to him, surprised. He seems about to say something, but in fear changes his mind.*

SOLOMON: Excuse me, go right ahead. *He goes nervously to his portfolio, reaching into it—which was not his original intention.* I'm sorry to disturb you. *He takes out an orange and starts back to the bedroom, then halts, addressing Walter*: About the harp. If you'll make me a straight out-and-out sale, I would be willing to go another fifty dollars. So it's eleven fifty, and between the two of you nobody has to do any favors.

WALTER: Well, you're getting warmer.

SOLOMON: I'm a fair person! So you don't have to bother with the appraisal and deductions, all right? *Before Walter can answer*: But don't rush, I'll wait. I'm at your service. *He goes quickly and worriedly into the bedroom.*

ESTHER, *starting to laugh; to Victor*: Where did you *find* him?

WALTER: —that wonderful? He "made it all ethical!"

> *Esther bursts out laughing, and Walter with her, and Victor manages to join. As it begins to subside, Walter turns to him.*

What do you say, Vic? Will you come by?

> *The laughter is gone. The smile is just fading on Victor's face. He looks at nothing, as though deciding. The pause lengthens, and lengthens still. Now it begins to seem he may not speak at all. No one knows how to break into his puzzling silence. At last he turns to Walter with a rather quick movement of his head as though he had made up his mind to take the step.*

VICTOR: I'm not sure I know what you want, Walter.

> *Walter looks shocked, astonished, almost unbelieving. But Victor's gaze is steady on him.*

ESTHER, *with a tone of the conciliator shrouding her shock and protest*: I don't think that's being very fair, is it?

VICTOR: Why is it unfair? We're talking about some pretty big steps here. *To Walter*: Not that I don't appreciate it, Walter, but certain things have happened, haven't they? *With a half laugh*: It just seems odd to suddenly be talking about—

WALTER, *downing his resentment*: I'd hoped we could take one step at a time, that's all. It's very complicated between us, I think, and it seemed to me we might just try to—

VICTOR: I know, but you can understand it would be a little confusing.

WALTER—*unwillingly, anger peaks his voice*: What do you find confusing?

VICTOR—*considers for a moment, but he cannot go back*: You must have some idea, don't you?

WALTER: This is a little astonishing, Victor. After all these years you can't expect to settle everything in one conversation, can you? I simply felt that with a little good will we . . . we . . . *He sees Victor's adamant poise*. Oh, the hell with it. *He goes abruptly and snatches up his coat and one of the evening gowns*. Get what you can from the old man, I don't want any of it. *He goes and extends his hand to Esther, forcing a smile*. I'm sorry, Esther. It was nice seeing you anyway.

> *Sickened, she accepts his hand.*

Maybe I'll see you again, Vic. Good luck. *He starts for the door. There are tears in his eyes.*

ESTHER, *before she can think*: Walter?

> *Walter halts and turns to her questioningly. She looks to Victor helplessly. But he cannot think either.*

WALTER: I don't accept this resentment, Victor. It simply baffles me. I don't understand it. I just want you to know how I feel.

ESTHER, *assuaging*: It's not resentment, Walter.

VICTOR: The whole thing is a little fantastic to me, that's all. I haven't cracked a book in twenty-five years, how do I walk into a research laboratory?

ESTHER: But Walter feels that you have enough background—

VICTOR, *almost laughing over his quite concealed anger at her*: I know less chemistry than most high-school kids, Esther. *To Walter*: And physics, yet! Good God, Walter. *He laughs*. Where you been?

WALTER: I'm sure you could make a place for yourself—

VICTOR: What place? Running papers from one office to another?

WALTER: You're not serious.

VICTOR: Why? Sooner or later my being your brother is not going to mean very much, is it? I've been walking a beat for twenty-eight years, I'm not qualified for anything technical. What's this all about?

WALTER: Why do you keep asking what it's about? I've been perfectly open with you, Victor!

VICTOR: I don't think you have.

WALTER: Why! What do you think I'm—?

VICTOR: Well, when you say what you said a few minutes ago, I—

WALTER: What did I say?!

VICTOR, *with a resolutely cool smile*: What a pity it was that I didn't go on with science.

WALTER, *puzzled*: What's wrong with that?

VICTOR, *laughing*: Oh, Walter, come on, now!

WALTER: But I feel that. I've always felt that.

VICTOR, *smiling still, and pointing at the center chair; a new reverberation sounds in his voice*: There used to be a man in that chair, staring into space. Don't you remember that?

WALTER: Very well, yes. I sent him money every month.

VICTOR: You sent him five dollars every month.

WALTER: I could afford five dollars. But what's that got to do with you?

VICTOR: What it's got to do with me!

WALTER: Yes, I don't see that.

VICTOR: Where did you imagine the rest of his living was coming from?

WALTER: Victor, that was your decision, not mine.

VICTOR: My decision!

WALTER: We had a long talk in this room once, Victor.

VICTOR, *not recalling*: What talk?

WALTER, *astonished*: Victor! We came to a complete under-standing—just after you moved up here with Dad. I told you then that I was going to finish my schooling come hell or high water, and I advised you to do the same. In fact, I warned you not to allow him to strangle your life. *To*

Esther: And if I'm not mistaken I told you the same at your wedding, Esther.

VICTOR, *with an incredulous laugh*: Who the hell was supposed to keep him alive, Walter?

WALTER, *with a strange fear, more than anger*: Why did anybody have to? He wasn't sick. He was perfectly fit to go to work.

VICTOR: Work? In 1936? With no skill, no money?

WALTER—*outburst*: Then he could have gone on welfare! Who *was* he, some exiled royalty? What did a hundred and fifty million other people do in 1936? He'd have survived, Victor. Good God, you must know that by now, don't you?!

    Slight pause.

VICTOR—*suddenly at the edge of fury, and caught by Walter's voicing his own opinion, he turns to Esther*: I've had enough of this, Esther; it's the same old thing all over again, let's get out of here. *He starts rapidly upstage toward the bedroom.*

WALTER, *quickly*: Vic! Please! *He catches Victor, who frees his arm.* I'm not running him down. I loved him in many ways—

ESTHER, *as though conceding her earlier position*: Vic, listen —maybe you *ought* to talk about it.

VICTOR: It's all pointless! The whole thing doesn't matter to me! *He turns to go to the bedroom.*

WALTER: He exploited you!

    Victor halts, turns to him, his anger full in his face.

Doesn't that matter to you?

VICTOR: Let's get one thing straight, Walter—I am nobody's victim.

WALTER: But that's exactly what I've tried to tell you. I'm not trying to condescend.

VICTOR: Of course you are. Would you be saying any of this if I'd made a pile of money somewhere? *Dead stop.* I'm sorry, Walter, I can't take that. I made no choice; the icebox was empty and the man was sitting there with his mouth open. *Slight pause.* I didn't start this, Walter, and the whole thing doesn't interest me, but when you talk about making choices, and I should have gone on with science, I have to say something.—Just because you want things a certain way doesn't make them that way. *He has ended at a point distant from Walter.*

> *A slight pause.*

WALTER, *with affront mixed into his trepidation*: All right then . . . How do *you* see it?

VICTOR: Look, you've been sick, Walter, why upset yourself with all this?

WALTER: It's important to me!

VICTOR, *trying to smile—and in a friendly way*: But why? It's all over the dam. *He starts toward the bedroom again.*

ESTHER: I think he's come to you in good faith, Victor.

> *He turns to her angrily, but she braves his look.*

I don't see why you can't consider his offer.

VICTOR: I said I'd consider it.

ESTHER, *restraining a cry*: You know you're turning it down!

In a certain fear of him, but persisting: I mean what's so dreadful about telling the truth, can it be any worse than this?

VICTOR: What "truth?" What are you—?

Solomon suddenly appears from the bedroom.

ESTHER: For God's sake, *now* what?

SOLOMON: I just didn't want you to think I wouldn't make the appraisal; I will, I'll do it—

ESTHER, *pointing to the bedroom*: Will you please leave us alone!

SOLOMON, *suddenly, his underlying emotion coming through; indicating Victor*: What do you want from him! He's a policeman! I'm a dealer, he's a doctor, and he's a policeman, so what's the good you'll tear him to pieces?!

ESTHER: Well, one of us has got to leave this room, Victor.

SOLOMON: Please, Esther, let me . . . *Going quickly to Walter*: Doctor, listen to me, take my advice—stop it. What can come of this? In the first place, if you take the deduction how do you know in two, three years they wouldn't come back to you, whereby they disallow it? I don't have to tell you, the Federal Government is not reliable. I understand very well you want to be sweet to him—*to Esther*—but can be two, three years before you'll know how sweet they're going to allow him. *To Victor and Walter*: In other words, what I'm trying to bring out, my boys, is that—

ESTHER: —you want the furniture.

SOLOMON, *shouting at her*: Esther, if I didn't want it I wouldn't buy it! But what can they settle here? It's still up to the Federal Government, don't you see? If they can't settle nothing they should stop it right now! *With a look of warning and alarm in his eyes*: Now please—do what I tell you! I'm not a fool! *He walks out into the bedroom, shaking.*

WALTER: *after a moment*: I guess he's got a point, Vic. Why don't you just sell it to him; maybe then we can sit down and talk sometime. *Glancing at the furniture*: It isn't really a very conducive atmosphere.—Can I call you?

VICTOR: Sure.

ESTHER: You're both fantastic. *She tries to laugh.* We're giving this furniture away because nobody's able to say the simplest things. You're incredible, the both of you.

WALTER, *a little shamed*: It isn't that easy, Esther.

ESTHER: Oh, what the hell—I'll say it. When he went to you, Walter, for the five hundred he needed to get his degree—

VICTOR: Esther! There's no—

ESTHER: It's one of the things standing between you, isn't it? Maybe Walter can clear it up. I mean . . . Good God, is there never to be an end? *To Walter, without pause*: Because it stunned him, Walter. He'll never say it, but—*she takes the plunge*—he hadn't the slightest doubt you'd lend it to him. So when you turned him down—

VICTOR, *as though it wearies him*: Esther, he was just starting out—

ESTHER, *in effect, taking her separate road*: Not the way you told me! Please let me finish! *To Walter*: You already had the house in Rye, you were perfectly well established, weren't you?

VICTOR: So what? He didn't feel he could—

WALTER, *with a certain dread, quietly*: No, no, I . . . I could have spared the money . . . *He sits slowly.* Please, Vic— sit down, it'll only take a moment.

VICTOR: I just don't see any point in—

WALTER: No—no; maybe it's just as well to talk now. We've never talked about this. I think perhaps we have to. *Slight pause. Toward Esther*: It *was* despicable; but I don't think I can leave it quite that way. *Slight pause.* Two or three days afterward—*to Victor*—after you came to see me, I phoned to offer you the money. Did you know that?

> *Slight pause.*

VICTOR: Where'd you phone?

WALTER: Here. I spoke to Dad.

> *Slight pause. Victor sits.*

I saw that I'd acted badly, and I—

VICTOR: You didn't act badly—

WALTER, *with a sudden flight of his voice*: It was frightful! *He gathers himself against his past.* We'll have another talk, won't we? I wasn't prepared to go into all this. . . .

> *Victor is expressionless.*

In any case . . . when I called here he told me you'd joined the Force. And I said—he mustn't permit you to do a thing like that. I said—you had a fine mind and with a little luck you could amount to something in science. That it was a terrible waste. Etcetera. And his answer was—"Victor wants to help me. I can't stop him."

> *Pause.*

VICTOR: You told him you were ready to give me the money?

WALTER: Victor, you remember the . . . the helplessness in his voice. At that time? With Mother recently gone and everything shot out from under him?

VICTOR, *persisting*: Let me understand that, Walter; did you tell—?

WALTER, *in anguish, but hewing to himself*: There are conversations, aren't there, and looking back it's impossible to explain why you said or didn't say certain things? I'm not defending it, but I would like to be understood, if that's possible. You all seemed to need each other more, Vic—more than I needed them. I was never able to feel your kind of . . . faith in him; that . . . confidence. His selfishness—which was perfectly normal—was always obvious to me, but you never seemed to notice it. To the point where I used to blame myself for a lack of feeling. You understand? So when he said that you wanted to help him, I felt somehow that it'd be wrong for me to try to break it up between you. It seemed like interfering.

VICTOR: I see.—Because he never mentioned you'd offered the money.

WALTER: All I'm trying to convey is that . . . I was never indifferent; that's the whole point. I did call here to offer the loan, but he made it impossible, don't you see?

VICTOR: I understand.

WALTER, *eagerly*: Do you?

VICTOR: Yes.

WALTER, *sensing the unsaid*: Please say what you think. It's absurd to go on this way. What do you want to say?

VICTOR—*slight pause*: I think it was all . . . very convenient for you.

WALTER, *appalled*: That's all?

VICTOR: I think so. If you thought Dad meant so much to me—and I guess he did in a certain way—why would five hundred bucks break us apart? I'd have gone on supporting him; it would have let me finish school, that's all.—It doesn't make any sense, Walter.

WALTER, *with a hint of hysteria in his tone*: What makes sense?

VICTOR: You didn't give me the money because you didn't want to.

WALTER, *hurt and quietly enraged—slight pause*: It's that simple.

VICTOR: That's what it comes to, doesn't it? Not that you had any obligation, but if you want to help somebody you do it, if you don't you don't. *He sees Walter's growing frustration and Esther's impatience.* Well, why is that so astonishing? We do what we want to do, don't we? *Walter doesn't reply. Victor's anxiety rises.* I don't understand what you're bringing this all up for.

WALTER: You don't feel the need to heal anything.

VICTOR: I wouldn't mind that, but how does this heal anything?

ESTHER: I think he's been perfectly clear, Victor. He's asking your friendship.

VICTOR: By offering me a job and twelve thousand dollars?

WALTER: Why not? What else can I offer you?

VICTOR: But why do you have to offer me anything?

Walter is silent, morally checked.

It sounds like I have to be saved, or something.

WALTER: I simply felt that there was work you could do that you'd enjoy and I—

VICTOR: Walter, I haven't got the education, what are you talking about? You can't walk in with one splash and wash out twenty-eight years. There's a price people pay. I've paid it, it's all gone, I haven't got it any more. Just like you paid, didn't you? You've got no wife, you've lost your family, you're rattling around all over the place? Can you go home and start all over again from scratch? This is where we are; now, right here, now. And as long as we're talking, I have to tell you that this is not what you say in front of a man's wife.

WALTER, *glancing at Esther, certainty shattered*: What have I said . . . ?

VICTOR, *trying to laugh*: We don't need to be saved, Walter! I've done a job that has to be done and I think I've done it straight. You talk about being out of the rat race, in my opinion, you're in it as deep as you ever were. Maybe more.

ESTHER—*stands*: I want to go, Victor.

VICTOR: Please, Esther, he's said certain things and I don't think I can leave it this way.

ESTHER, *angrily*: Well, what's the difference?

VICTOR, *suppressing an outburst*: Because for some reason you don't understand *anything* any more! *He is trembling as he turns to Walter.* What are you trying to tell me—that it was all unnecessary? Is that it?

Walter is silent.

Well, correct me, is that the message? Because that's all I get out of this.

WALTER, *toward Esther*: I guess it's impossible—

VICTOR, *the more strongly because Walter seems about to be allied with Esther*: What's impossible? . . . What do you *want,* Walter!

WALTER—*in the pause is the admission that he indeed has not leveled yet. And there is fear in his voice*: I wanted to be of some use. I've learned some painful things, but it isn't enough to know; I wanted to act on what I know.

VICTOR: Act—in what way?

WALTER, *knowing it may be a red flag, but his honor is up*: I feel . . . I could be of help. Why live, only to repeat the same mistakes again and again? I didn't want to let the chance go by, as I let it go before.

> *Victor is unconvinced.*

And I must say, if this is as far as you can go with me, then you're only defeating yourself.

VICTOR: Like I did before.

> *Walter is silent.*

Is that what you mean?

WALTER—*hesitates, then with frightened but desperate acceptance of combat*: All right, yes; that's what I meant.

VICTOR: Well, that's what I thought.—See, there's one thing about the cops—you get to learn how to listen to people, because if you don't hear right sometimes you end up with a knife in your back. In other words, I dreamed up the whole problem.

WALTER, *casting aside his caution, his character at issue*: Victor, my five hundred dollars was not what kept you from your degree! You could have left Pop and gone right on— he was perfectly fit.

VICTOR: And twelve million unemployed, what was that, my neurosis? I hypnotized myself every night to scrounge the outer leaves of lettuce from the Greek restaurant on the corner? The good parts we cut out of rotten grapefruit . . . ?

WALTER: I'm not trying to deny—

VICTOR, *leaning into Walter's face*: We were eating garbage here, buster!

ESTHER: But what is the point of—

VICTOR, *to Esther*: What are you trying to do, turn it all into a dream? *To Walter*: And perfectly fit! What about the inside of his head? The man was ashamed to go into the street!

ESTHER: But Victor, he's gone now.

VICTOR, *with a cry—he senses the weakness of his position*: Don't tell me he's gone now! *He is wracked, terribly alone before her*. He was here then, wasn't he? And a system broke down, did I invent that?

ESTHER: No, dear, but it's all different now.

VICTOR: What's different now? We're a goddamned army holding this city down and when it blows again you'll be thankful for a roof over your head! *To Walter*: How can you say that to me? I could have left him with your five dollars a month? I'm sorry, you can't brainwash me—if you got a hook in your mouth don't try to stick it into mine. You want to make up for things, you don't come around to make fools out of people. I didn't invent my life. Not altogether. You had a responsibility here and you walked on it. . . . You can go. I'll send you your half.

He is across the room from Walter, his face turned away. A long pause.

WALTER: If you can reach beyond anger, I'd like to tell you something. Vic? *Victor does not move.* I know I should have said this many years ago. But I did try. When you came to me I told you—remember I said, "Ask Dad for money"? I did say that.

Pause.

VICTOR: What are you talking about?

WALTER: He had nearly four thousand dollars.

ESTHER: When?

WALTER: When they were eating garbage here.

Pause.

VICTOR: How do you know that?

WALTER: He'd asked me to invest it for him.

VICTOR: Invest it.

WALTER: Yes. Not long before he sent you to me for the loan.

Victor is silent.

That's why I never sent him more than I did. And if I'd had the strength of my convictions I wouldn't have sent him that!

Victor sits down in silence. A shame is flooding into him which he struggles with. He looks at nobody.

VICTOR, *as though still absorbing the fact*: He actually had it? In the bank?

WALTER: Vic, that's what he was living on, basically, till he died. What we gave him wasn't enough; you know that.

VICTOR: But he had those jobs—

WALTER: Meant very little. He lived on his money, believe me. I told him at the time, if he would send you through I'd contribute properly. But here he's got you running from job to job to feed him—I'm damned if I'd sacrifice when he was holding out on you. You can understand that, can't you?

Victor turns to the center chair and, shaking his head, exhales a blow of anger and astonishment.

Kid, there's no point getting angry now. You know how terrified he was that he'd never earn anything any more. And there was just no reassuring him.

VICTOR, *with protest—it is still nearly incredible*: But he saw I was supporting him, didn't he?

WALTER: For how long, though?

VICTOR, *angering*: What do you mean, how long? He could see I wasn't walking out—

WALTER: I know, but he was sure you would sooner or later.

ESTHER: He was waiting for him to walk out.

WALTER—*fearing to inflame Victor, he undercuts the obvious answer*: Well . . . you could say that, yes.

ESTHER: I knew it! God, when do I believe what I see!

WALTER: He was terrified, dear, and . . . *To Victor*: I don't mean that he wasn't grateful to you, but he really couldn't understand it. I may as well say it, Vic—I myself never imagined you'd go that far.

> *Victor looks at him. Walter speaks with delicacy in the face of a possible explosion.*

Well, you must certainly see now how extreme a thing it was, to stick with him like that? And at such cost to you?

> *Victor is silent.*

ESTHER, *with sorrow*: He sees it.

WALTER, *to erase it all, to achieve the reconciliation*: We could work together, Vic. I know we could. And I'd love to try it. What do you say?

> *There is a long pause. Victor now glances at Esther to see her expression. He sees she wants him to. He is on the verge of throwing it all up. Finally he turns to Walter, a new note of awareness in his voice.*

VICTOR: Why didn't you tell me he had that kind of money?

WALTER: But I did when you came to me for the loan.

VICTOR: To "ask Dad"?

WALTER: Yes!

VICTOR: But would I have come to you if I had the faintest idea he had four thousand dollars under his ass? It was meaningless to say that to me.

WALTER: Now just a second . . . *He starts to indicate the harp.*

VICTOR: Cut it out, Walter! I'm sorry, but it's kind of insulting. I'm not five years old! What am I supposed to make of this? You knew he had that kind of money, and came here many times, you sat here, the two of you, watching me walking around in this suit? And now you expect me to—?

WALTER, *sharply*: You certainly knew he had *something*, Victor!

VICTOR: What do you want here? What do you want here!

WALTER: Well, all I can tell you is that *I* wouldn't sit around eating garbage with *that* staring me in the face! *He points at the harp.* Even then it was worth a couple of hundred, maybe more! Your degree was right there. Right there, if nothing else.

> *Victor is silent, trembling.*

But if you want to go on with this fantasy, it's all right with me. God knows, I've had a few of my own.

> *He starts for his coat.*

VICTOR: Fantasy.

WALTER: It's a fantasy, Victor. Your father was penniless and your brother a son of a bitch, and you play no part at all. I said to ask him because you could see in front of your face that he had some money. You knew it then and you certainly know it now.

VICTOR: You mean if he had a few dollars left, that—?

ESTHER: What do you mean, a few dollars?

VICTOR, *trying to retract*: I didn't know he—

ESTHER: But you knew he had something?

VICTOR, *caught; as though in a dream where nothing is explicable*: I didn't say that.

ESTHER: Then what are you saying?

VICTOR, *pointing at Walter*: Don't you have anything to say to *him*?

ESTHER: I want to understand what you're saying! You knew he had money left?

VICTOR: Not four thousand dol—

ESTHER: But enough to make out?

VICTOR, *crying out in anger and for release*: I couldn't nail him to the wall, could I? He said he had nothing!

ESTHER, *stating and asking*: But you knew better.

VICTOR: I don't know what I knew! *He has called this out, and his voice and words surprise him. He sits staring, cornered by what he senses in himself.*

ESTHER: It's a farce. It's all a goddamned farce!

VICTOR: Don't. Don't say that.

ESTHER: Farce! To stick us into a furnished room so you could send him part of your pay? Even after we were married, to go on sending him money? Put off having children, live like mice—and all the time you knew he . . . ? Victor, I'm trying to understand you. Victor?—Victor!

VICTOR, *roaring out, agonized*: Stop it! Silence. *Then*: Jesus, you can't leave everything out like this. The man was a beaten dog, ashamed to walk in the street, how do you demand his last buck—?

ESTHER: You're still saying that? The man had *four thousand dollars!*

> *He is silent.*

It was all an act! Beaten dog!—he was a calculating liar! And in your heart you knew it!

> *He is struck silent by the fact, which is still ungraspable.*

No wonder you're paralyzed—you haven't believed a word you've said all these years We've been lying away our existence all these years; down the sewer, day after day after day . . . to protect a miserable cheap manipulator. No wonder it all seemed like a dream to me—it *was;* a goddamned nightmare. I knew it was all unreal, I knew it and I let it go by. Well, I can't any more, kid. I can't watch it another day. *I'm* not ready to die. *She moves toward her purse.*

> *She sits. Pause.*

VICTOR—*not going to her; he can't. He is standing yards from her.* This isn't true either.

ESTHER: We are dying, that's what's true!

VICTOR: I'll tell you what happened. You want to hear it? *She catches the lack of advocacy in his tone, the simplicity. He moves from her, gathering himself, and glances at the center chair, then at Walter.* I did tell him what you'd said to me. I faced him with it. *He doesn't go on; his eyes go to the chair.* Not that I "faced" him, I just told him—"Walter said to ask you." *He stops; his stare is on the center chair, caught by memory; in effect, the last line was addressed to the chair.*

WALTER: And what happened?

Pause.

VICTOR, *quietly*: He laughed. I didn't know what to make of it. Tell you the truth—*to Esther*—I don't think a week has gone by that I haven't seen that laugh. Like it was some kind of a wild joke—because we *were* eating garbage here. *He breaks off.* I didn't know what I was supposed to do. And I went out. I went—*he sits, staring*—over to Bryant Park behind the public library. *Slight pause.* The grass was covered with men. Like a battlefield; a big open-air flophouse. And not bums—some of them still had shined shoes and good hats, busted businessmen, lawyers, skilled mechanics. Which I'd seen a hundred times. But suddenly— you know?—I *saw* it. *Slight pause.* There was no mercy. Anywhere. *Glancing at the chair at the end of the table*: One day you're the head of the house, at the head of the table, and suddenly you're shit. Overnight. And I tried to figure out that laugh.—How could he be holding out on me when he loved me?

ESTHER: Loved . . .

VICTOR, *his voice swelling with protest*: He loved me, Esther! He just didn't want to end up on the grass! It's not that you don't love somebody, it's that you've got to survive. We know what that feels like, don't we!

She can't answer, feeling the barb.

We do what we have to do. *With a wide gesture including her and Walter and himself*: What else are we talking about here? If he did have something left it was—

ESTHER: *"If"* he had—

VICTOR: What does that change! I know I'm talking like a fool, but what does that change? He couldn't believe in anybody any more, and it was unbearable to me! *The unlooked-for return of his old feelings seems to anger him. Of Walter:* He'd kicked him in the face; my mother—*he glances toward Walter as he speaks; there is hardly a pause*—the night he told us he was bankrupt, my mother . . . It was right on this couch. She was all dressed up—for some affair, I think. Her hair was piled up, and long earrings? And he had his tuxedo on . . . and made us all sit down; and he told us it was all gone. And she vomited. *Slight pause. His horror and pity twist in his voice.* All over his arms. His hands. Just kept on vomiting, like thirty-five years coming up. And he sat there. Stinking like a sewer. And a look came onto his face. I'd never seen a man look like that. He was sitting there, letting it dry on his hands. *Pause. He turns to Esther.* What's the difference what you know? Do *you* do everything you know?

She avoids his eyes, his mourning shared.

Not that I excuse it; it was idiotic, nobody has to tell me that. But you're brought up to believe in one another, you're filled full of that crap—you can't help trying to keep it going, that's all. I thought if I stuck with him, if he could see that somebody was still . . . *He breaks off; the reason strangely has fallen loose. He sits.* I can't explain it; I wanted to . . . stop it from falling apart. I . . . *He breaks off again, staring.*

Pause.

WALTER, *quietly:* It won't work, Vic.

Victor looks at him, then Esther does.

You see it yourself, don't you? It's not that at all. You see that, don't you?

VICTOR, *quietly, avidly*: What?

WALTER, *with his driving need*: Is it really that something fell apart? Were we really brought up to believe in one another? We were brought up to succeed, weren't we? Why else would he respect me so and not you? What fell apart? What was here to fall apart?

Victor looks away at the burgeoning vision.

Was there ever any love here? When he needed her, she vomited. And when you needed him, he laughed. What was unbearable is not that it all fell apart, it was that there was never anything here.

Victor turns back to him, fear on his face.

ESTHER, *as though she herself were somehow moving under the rays of judgment*: But who . . . who can ever face that, Walter?

WALTER, *to her*: You have to! *To Victor*: What you saw behind the library was not that there was no mercy in the world, kid. It's that there was no love in this house. There was no loyalty. There was nothing here but a straight financial arrangement. That's what was unbearable. And you proceeded to wipe out what you saw.

VICTOR, *with terrible anxiety*: Wipe out—

WALTER: Vic, I've been in this box. I wasted thirty years protecting myself from that catastrophe. *He indicates the chair*: And I only got out alive when I saw that there was no catastrophe, there had never been. They were never lovers—she said a hundred times that her marriage destroyed her musical career. I saw that nothing fell here, Vic—and he doesn't follow me any more with that vomit on his hands. I don't look high and low for some betrayal any more; my days belong to *me* now, I'm not afraid to risk believing some-one. All I ever wanted was simply to do science, but I invented an efficient, disaster-proof, money-maker. You— *to Esther, with a warm smile*: He could never stand the sight of blood. He was shy, he was sensitive . . . *To Victor*: And what do you do? March straight into the most violent profession there is. We invent ourselves, Vic, to wipe out what we know. You invent a life of self-sacrifice, a life of duty; but what never existed here cannot be upheld. You were not upholding something, you were denying what you knew they were. And denying yourself. And that's all that is standing between us now—an illusion, Vic. That I kicked them in the face and you must uphold them against me. But I only saw then what you see now—there was nothing here to betray. I am not your enemy. It is all an illusion and if you could walk through it, we could meet . . . *His reconciliation is on him*. You see why I said before, that in the hospital—when it struck me so that we . . . we're brothers. It was only two seemingly different roads out of the same trap. It's almost as though—*he smiles warmly, uncertain still*—we're like two halves of the same guy. As though we can't quite move ahead—alone. You ever feel that?

> *Victor is silent.*

Vic?

> *Pause.*

VICTOR: Walter, I'll tell you—there are days when I can't remember what I've got against you. *He laughs emptily, in suffering*. It hangs in me like a rock. And I see myself in a store window, and my hair going, I'm walking the streets —and I can't remember why. And you can go crazy trying to figure it out when all the reasons disappear—when you can't even hate any more.

WALTER: Because it's unreal, Vic, and underneath you know it is.

VICTOR: Then give me something real.

WALTER: What can I give you?

VICTOR: I'm not blaming you now, I'm asking you. I can understand you walking out. I've wished a thousand times I'd done the same thing. But, to come here through all those years knowing what you knew and saying nothing . . .?

WALTER: And if I said—Victor, if I said that I did have some wish to hold you back? What would that give you now?

VICTOR: Is that what you wanted? Walter, tell me the truth.

WALTER: I wanted the freedom to do my work. Does that mean I stole your life? *Crying out and standing*: You made those choices, Victor! And that's what you have to face!

VICTOR: But, what do you face? You're not turning me into a walking fifty-year-old mistake—we have to go home when you leave, we have to look at each other. What do *you* face?

WALTER: I have offered you everything I know how to!

VICTOR: I would know if you'd come to give me something! I would know that!

WALTER, *crossing for his coat*: You don't want the truth, you want a monster!

VICTOR: You came for the old handshake, didn't you! The okay!

Walter halts in the doorway.

And you end up with the respect, the career, the money, and the best of all, the thing that nobody else can tell you so you can believe it—that you're one hell of a guy and never harmed anybody in your life! Well, you won't get it, not till I get mine!

WALTER: And you? You never had any hatred for me? Never a wish to see me destroyed? To destroy me, to destroy me with this saintly self-sacrifice, this mockery of sacrifice? What will you give me, Victor?

VICTOR: I don't have it to give you. Not any more. And you don't have it to give me. And there's nothing to give— I see that now. I just didn't want him to end up on the grass. And he didn't. That's all it was, and I don't need anything more. I couldn't work with you, Walter. I can't. I don't trust you.

WALTER: Vengeance. Down to the end. *To Esther*: He is sacrificing his life to vengeance.

ESTHER: Nothing was sacrificed.

WALTER, *to Victor*: To prove with your failure what a treacherous son of a bitch I am!—to hang yourself in my doorway!

ESTHER: Leave him, Walter—please, don't say any more!

WALTER—*humiliated by her. He is furious. He takes an unplanned step toward the door*: You quit; both of you. *To Victor as well*: You lay down and quit, and that's the long and short of all your ideology. It is all envy!

> *Solomon enters, apprehensive, looks from one to the other.*

And to this moment you haven't the guts to face it! But your failure does not give you moral authority! Not with me! I *worked* for what I made and there are people walking around today who'd have been dead if I hadn't. Yes. *Moving toward the door, he points at the center chair.* He was smarter than all of us—he saw what you wanted and he gave it to you! *He suddenly reaches out and grabs Solomon's face and laughs.* Go ahead, you old mutt—rob them blind, they love it! *Letting go, he turns to Victor.* You will never, never again make me ashamed! *He strides toward the doorway. A gown lies on the dining table, spread out, and he is halted in surprise at the sight of it.*

> *Suddenly Walter sweeps it up in his hands and rushes at Victor, flinging the gown at him with an outcry. Victor backs up at his wild approach.*

VICTOR: Walter!

> *The flicker of a humiliated smile passes across Walter's face. He wants to disappear into air. He turns, hardly glancing at Victor, makes for the door, and, straightening, goes out.*

VICTOR—*starts hesitantly to the door*: Maybe he oughtn't go into the street like that—

SOLOMON, *stopping him with his hand*: Let him go.

> *Victor turns to Solomon uncertainly.*

What can you do?

ESTHER: Whatever you see, huh.

> *Solomon turns to her, questioningly.*

You believe what you see.

SOLOMON, *thinking she was rebuking him*: What then?

ESTHER: No—it's wonderful. Maybe that's why you're still going.

Victor turns to her. She stares at the doorway.

I was nineteen years old when I first walked up those stairs —if that's believable. And he had a brother, who was the cleverest, most wonderful young doctor . . . in the world. As he'd be soon. Somehow, some way. *She turns to the center chair.* And a rather sweet, inoffensive gentleman, always waiting for the news to come on. . . . And next week, men we never saw or heard of will come and smash it all apart and take it all away.—So many times I thought—the one thing he wanted most was to talk to his brother, and that if they could— But he's come and he's gone. And I still feel it—isn't that terrible? It always seems to me that one little step more and some crazy kind of forgiveness will come and lift up everyone. When do you stop being so . . . foolish?

SOLOMON: I had a daughter, should rest in peace, she took her own life. That's nearly fifty years. And every night I lay down to sleep, she's sitting there. I see her clear like I see you. But if it was a miracle and she came to life, what would I say to her? *He turns back to Victor, paying out.* So you got there seven; so I'm giving you eight, nine, ten, eleven— *he searches, finds a fifty*—and there's a fifty for the harp. Now you'll excuse me—I got a lot of work here tonight. *He gets his pad and pencil and begins carefully listing each piece.*

VICTOR—*folds the money*: We could still make the picture, if you like.

ESTHER: Okay.

> *He goes to his suit and begins to rip the plastic wrapper off.*

Don't bother.

He looks at her.

She turns to Solomon. Goodbye, Mr. Solomon.

SOLOMON—*looks up from his pad*: Goodbye, dear. I like that suit, that's very nice. *He returns to his work.*

ESTHER: Thank you. *She walks out with her life.*

VICTOR—*buckles on his gun belt, pulls up his tie*: When will you be taking it away?

SOLOMON: With God's help if I'll live, first thing in the morning.

VICTOR, *of the suit*: I'll be back for this later, then. And there's my foil, and the mask, and the gauntlets. *Puts on his uniform jacket.*

SOLOMON, *continuing his work*: Don't worry, I wouldn't touch it.

VICTOR, *extending his hand*: I'm glad to have met you, Solomon.

SOLOMON: Likewise. And I want to thank you.

VICTOR: What for?

SOLOMON, *with a glance at the furniture*: Well . . . who would ever believe I would start such a thing again . . . ? *He cuts himself off.* But go, go, I got a lot of work here.

VICTOR, *starting to the door, putting his cap on*: Good luck with it.

SOLOMON: Good luck you can never know till the last minute, my boy.

VICTOR, *smiling*: Right. Yes. *With a last look around at the room.* Well . . . bye-bye.

SOLOMON, *as Victor goes out*: Bye-bye, bye-bye.

> *He is alone. He has the pad and pencil in his hand, and he takes the pencil to start work again. But he looks about, and the challenge of it all oppresses him and he is afraid and worried. His hand goes to his cheek, he pulls his flesh in fear, his eyes circling the room.*

> *His eye falls on the phonograph. He goes, inspects it, winds it up, sets the tone arm on the record, and flicks the starting lever. The Laughing Record plays. As the two comedians begin their routine, his depressed expression gives way to surprise. Now he smiles. He chuckles, and remembers. Now a laugh escapes, and he nods his head in recollection. He is laughing now, and shakes his head back and forth as though to say, "It still works!" And the laughter, of the record and his own, increase and combine. He holds his head, unable to stop laughing, and sits in the center chair. He leans back sprawling in the chair, laughing with tears in his eyes, howling helplessly to the air.*

SLOW CURTAIN

AUTHOR'S PRODUCTION NOTE

A fine balance of sympathy should be maintained in the playing of the roles of Victor and Walter. The actor playing Walter must not regard his attempts to win back Victor's friendship as mere manipulation. From entrance to exit, Walter is attempting to put into action what he has learned about himself, and sympathy will be evoked for him in proportion to the openness, the depth of need, the intimations of suffering with which the role is played.

This admonition goes beyond the question of theatrics to the theme of the play. As the world now operates, the qualities of both brothers are necessary to it; surely their respective psychologies and moral values conflict at the heart of the social dilemma. The production must therefore withhold judgment in favor of presenting both men in all their humanity and from their own viewpoints. Actually, each has merely proved to the other what the other has known but dared not face. At the end, demanding of one another what was forfeited to time, each is left touching the structure of his life.

The play can be performed with an intermission, as indicated at the end of Act One, if circumstances require it. But an unbroken performance is preferable.

The play was directed by Ulu Grosbard and produced by Robert Whitehead. It opened on February 7, 1968, at the Morosco Theatre, New York City.

THE CAST
(in order of appearance)

VICTOR FRANZ	Pat Hingle
ESTHER FRANZ	Kate Reid
GREGORY SOLOMON	Harold Gary
WALTER FRANZ	Arthur Kennedy